IF YE CONTINUE

IF YE CONTINUE

GUY DUTY

BETHANY FELLOWSHIP, INC. ■ MINNEAPOLIS, MINNESOTA

*Printed in the United States of America
by the Printing Division of Bethany Fellowship, Inc.
Minneapolis, Minnesota*

DEDICATED

to those librarians who have shown
much kindness in helping me in my
studies and researches in their libraries

Contents

Introduction

AMONG ALL MY MINISTER FRIENDS, I know one in particular who had experienced a long and serious conflict over the doctrine of Eternal Security while a student at a Calvinist university. Knowing of his lengthy struggle with the doctrine, I asked him to read the manuscript for this book. He kindly did so, and wrote me:

> I have just gone through your pages, and I have never read anything like it or as good. Your book *God's Covenants and Our Time* is excellent, but in this one you have really broken loose with inspiration.
>
> I came in contact with this teaching of Eternal Security while overseas during World War II. This first brush with Eternal Security gave me reason to give much private thought to the subject, "Once in grace, always in grace." However, I was totally unprepared for the bombshell explosion I faced when, after leaving the service, I enrolled in one of the largest fundamental Christian universities in America.
>
> I then found myself, a young divinity student, son of a very fundamental pastor, standing in the shadows of a doctrine which, if I accepted it, would change my entire belief. I desired to be open-minded enough to believe it if it were correct, even though it would mean changing my denomination.

Two of my roommates were well schooled in this "Once saved, always saved" teaching, and for months I tried to reason and debate with them as best I could. I wrote to my pastor and my father, asking them to send me everything they could find that might be of help. I sat in the offices of several of my professors asking questions and earnestly trying to find something that would help me.

In the years since that time, I have read every book and article I could find on both views of this subject and I concluded that all of them are convincing *if* you happen to believe the same as the author.

I have finished reading the manuscript for your new book, *If Ye Continue,* and at the close of each chapter I could only say, "If only I could have had this material at the university." You have approached this subject from a very refreshing angle. This scholarly work not only faces the arguments of Eternal Security teachers squarely, but proves from the Scriptures that salvation is conditional and is based solely on the fact that the believer must continue to believe.

The last few paragraphs of chapter 8 thrilled me as I read them. It reminded me of the months of great struggle I had with the same verses. I am very grateful for this fine book, and any open-minded reader must admit that it is completely Scriptural and unbiased in its views.

I believe this to be the most complete treatment of this subject written, and I would highly recommend it to every Bible student. Anyone reading this book must admit that it is the work of a great student of the Scriptures who has made every effort to "rightly divide the word of truth."

> Pastor Hartley Wigfield, Jr.
> Winchester, Virginia

My thanks to Pastor Wigfield for his review of my manuscript. I also owe much appreciation to Miss Mary Kibbe, a secretary who knows how to do it.

Various publishers kindly gave me permission to quote from their publications. They are named at the places of quotation.

The reader is requested to withhold judgment until he has read to the end, and then judge in fairness to the evidence presented.

Guy W. Duty

2

Statement of Purpose

Is SALVATION CONDITIONAL or unconditional?

This question has been a cause of stormy debate among Biblical interpreters for at least 16 centuries. It has divided the Christian world of theology since the days of the church fathers. Christian denominations today remain sharply divided over it. Doubtless the reader will agree that the truth on this question must be found on one side or the other. Truth is not a house divided against itself.

An impartial truth-seeker accepts facts as he finds them. He has no personal preference. I have no doctrinal preference for any subject taught in the Bible. Let truth be whatever it is about anything. If salvation is unconditional, then I desire to believe it; but we must have *proof* for our beliefs.

The literature on this subject is immense and highly conflicting. How shall we decide between the two sides? Both claim to be right. What is truth to one interpreter is error to another. Denominational teachers read a Bible text and get different ideas from it. How can we decide what is truth? What shall be the *standard of evidence* for our conclusion?

A Bible doctrine cannot be established merely by someone making a dogmatic statement. Doctrinal despots have done this for centuries. Even the church fathers were divided on conditional and unconditional salvation. How can we know who was right? —assuming that one was right. We respect the fathers but there was much in their writings that leave us on uncertain ground.

The Apostle Paul said, "Prove all things" (I Thess. 5:21), and nothing is more important than to prove our doctrines. So, there must be some way to prove them. If not, then we are adrift on a sea of hopeless confusion.

The point to be proved is whether salvation is conditional or unconditional. I take the position that it is conditional, and will present an array of evidence from Genesis to Revelation to prove it. Using the eight world-wide adopted rules of interpretation in the Appendix of this book, I will not only show that my interpretation satisfies all these rules but that the opposing interpretation violates them all.

With these rules of interpretation we shall see there is no contradiction in the Scriptures about salvation, but that the *whole* Bible is bound together in a harmonious *unit of truth* concerning it.

It will be helpful to a right understanding of this question to know a few historical facts that lie in the background. The origin and history of a doctrine are important to the proper understanding of it. Many eminent names are connected with this history but the four most prominent are Augustine, Pelagius, Calvin, and Arminius.

Augustine was a monk of the 5th century (354–430) in Africa. He is generally considered the greatest of the church fathers, and a theological genius. He was the dominant doctrinal authority of the Middle Ages, and his influence throughout the Christian world of theology has been enormous. He generally controlled the leaders of the church, and his influence extended for more than a thousand years.

Augustine's doctrine of predestination may be briefly expressed in the following quotations: [1]

> Before the creation of the world, God formed the resolution to redeem certain men in Christ and to apply to them his grace. There is a "good pleasure of his [God's] will," which has nothing to do with human merits, not even with such as were foreseen by God. On the contrary, the determination (propositum) of God is the ground upon which the good will is imparted to this or that one.... Predestination is the *cause* of salvation. All saving ordinances are means for realizing it, and therefore really serve and benefit only the predestinated.... Only to the elect comes the effectual "peculiar calling of the elect".... All, therefore, rests in the hands of God, depends upon his choice.

> Therefore, whoever have in the most provident ordering of God been foreknown, predestinated, called, justified...are now the sons of God and can by no means perish.

> The unpredestinated, or foreknown, on the other hand, under all circumstances, fall into ruin, as parts of the *massa perditionis*. Even if they appear to be real Christians, called, justified, regenerated through baptism, renewed—they will not be saved, because they are not elected. No blame attaches to God; they are alone to blame, as they simply remain given over to their just fate.

> He who falls, falls by his own will; and he who stands, stands by the will of God. In such God reveals his justice, as in the elect his mercy. No one is saved unless God wills it.

When Augustine was asked why God chooses some for salvation and leaves others for damnation, he replied that it was God's mysterious will, and that "the creature must bow humbly before his Creator." [2]

---

[1] *Textbook of the History of Doctrines*, Reinhold Seeberg, V. I, pp. 351, 352, 373. Baker, 1958.
[2] Ibid.

When Augustine was confronted with logical objections that exposed the "glaring defects" in his system of interpretation on predestination, he replied: "The more difficult this is to understand, the more laudable is the faith that believes it." [3]

We give due respect to Augustine, but a doctrine is not true because it is adorned with a great name. Augustine, "the oracle of 13 centuries," was guilty of violating major rules of interpretation in his predestination teaching.

Augustine had the serious weakness of other prejudiced interpreters. He specialized on those parts of Scripture that seemed to favor his position, but he twisted or ignored other parts that went against him. He laid down rules for his opponents on other doctrines, but he violated the same rules when teaching predestination. He warned others about the dangers of distorting the Scriptures, but he was guilty of constantly doing the same on the predestination Scriptures. Historians friendly to Augustine wrote:

> He was badly equipped for the work of exposition. He knew no Hebrew, and had but a meagre knowledge of Greek.... This is admitted even by his Benedictine editors.... His etymologies are terribly weak.[4]

> [There was] "a multitude of inconsistencies and self-contradictory tendencies in his teachings (e.g., predestination and church,... Christ and grace, grace and sacraments, the knowledge of God and the definition of God, faith, and love, et cetera).[5]

Some theologians followed the Augustinian ideas on predestination but others saw through his fallacies. Others partly accepted his theology and were

[3] Ibid.

[4] *History of Interpretation*, Farrar, F. W., p. 234. Baker, 1961.

[5] *Textbook of the History of Doctrines*, Reinhold Seeberg, V. 1, pp. 367–68. Baker, 1958.

called Semi-Augustinians. During the many-centuries history of this hotly debated doctrine, strong argumentation continued from both sides; but for many there was always something obscure, uncertain, and unclear about it. Confusion about the doctrine never ceased—nor has it to our day. Multitudes today cannot accept Augustine's dictum: "The more difficult this is to understand, the more laudable is the faith that believes it."

Augustine's chief opponent was a learned British monk named Pelagius, who also lived during the 5th century. He opposed Augustine's predestination and asserted the freedom of the human will to do good and evil.

He once led a theological disputation in Rome where he refuted the Augustinian doctrine of predestination and asserted the freedom of the will. He argued that as God had commanded men to do what is good, he must therefore have the ability to do it; that is, man is free and it is therefore possible for him to decide for or against that which is good. Freedom of the will consists in the possibility of committing sin or of abstaining from it. Man by nature is capable of good or evil but he must choose one or the other. Because of these views Pelagius was condemned and banished from Rome. Some theologians went half-way with Pelagius and were called Semi-Pelagians.

The Augustinian dispute continued for about 13 centuries to the time of a French theologian named John Calvin (1509–1564). In Geneva, Calvin was a pastor and professor of theology. He helped to establish a theocratic government there. Geneva was the center of defense of Protestantism throughout Europe. Calvin gathered and systematized the reformed theology of that period. Even his enemies admitted he was a brilliant theologian.

Calvin got his inspiration on predestination from Augustine. He developed Augustine's doctrine to a conclusion that is called, with other doctrinal points, "Calvinism." Today, Calvin's predestination is generally called "Eternal Security."

Calvin, like Augustine, defined predestination as God's eternal decree by which God's absolute sovereign will decided the eternal destiny of every individual. It was God's absolute predestinating purpose that determined who would be saved and who would be damned. Calvin admitted this was a "horrible decree," but argued that it was based on God's love and justice.

Calvin taught, like Augustine, that "man therefore falls, God's Providence so ordaining, but he falls by his own fault." He said that no cause for salvation was to be sought other than the absolute and unconditional will of God; and he said there was a deep mystery to this "horrible decree."

Calvin's writings on predestination greatly intensified the dispute. It raged back and forth among the theologians as it had for more than a thousand years. Synod after synod debated the doctrine but multitudes remained perplexed. There is widespread perplexity about it to this day.

I quote from Calvin's *Institutes*, Book 3, Chapter XXI.

> Predestination we call the decree of God, by which he has determined in Himself, what he would have to become of every individual of mankind. For they are not all created with a similar destiny: but eternal life is foreordained for some, and eternal damnation for others. Every man, therefore, being created for one or the other of these two ends, we say, he is predestinated either to life or death.

Calvin's meaning here is forcefully evident. The facts of language are clear. But, as we shall see later, Calvin, like Augustine, made inconsistent and self-contradictory statements. It seems to me that sometimes they were on both sides of the question. I do not see how anyone, especially those trained in precise analytical work, could get a clear and consistent picture of what they meant by predestination. Study their teachings thoroughly, analyze them, and even though you are an expert in language and logic, at times you will find yourself in a foggy world of words.

In contrast, the words of Scripture have a simplicity and clarity that even the "wayfaring man, and the fool [uneducated]" can understand. "If *thou* shalt confess with *thy* mouth the Lord Jesus, and shalt believe in *thine* heart that God hath raised him from the dead, *thou* shalt be saved" (Rom. 10:9). "*Whosoever* will, let him take the water of life freely" (Rev. 22:17).

Perhaps Augustine and Calvin didn't mean all that their opponents charge them with on predestination, but their teachings are so obscure and contradictory that perhaps no one could be blamed for being confused about their meaning. Paul said: "God is not the author of confusion" (I Cor. 14:33). Who then is the author of this doctrinal confusion in Christianity today?

It seems strange that Calvin, the law student, did not see the "multitude of inconsistencies and self-contradictory tendencies" in the Augustinian theology he adopted.

> Calvin, honest as he meant to be, found...the
> fatal facility of reading into Scripture what he
> wished to find there.[6]

I am not quoting from Calvin's enemies but from a historian friendly to him. Dean Farrar, an eminent

---

[6] *History of Interpretation*, Farrar, F. W., p. 351. Baker, 1961.

scholar, admitted that Calvin was one of the foremost interpreters of Scripture, but he also said:

> [Calvin] had a manner in which he explains away every passage which runs counter to his dogmatic pre-possessions.[7]

Some of Calvin's friends couldn't go all the way with him on predestination, and they were called Semi-Calvinists. Full-fledged Calvinists were Hyper-Calvinists. Many Calvinists today disagree about predestination.

As the Calvinist dispute continued, there appeared on the scene another important theologian named Arminius (1560–1609). He was a Dutch pastor. At first he defended the views of Calvin, but further study caused him to adopt the beliefs of Calvin's opponents. He engaged in bitter arguments about Calvinism, rejecting the Augustinian-Calvinistic doctrine of absolute predestination and taught conditional predestination. He was a powerful influence against Calvinism, and his influence extends to our day.

During the many-centuries dispute about the doctrine, confusion was widespread. Perplexity never ceased, nor has it to our time. In an effort to settle the dispute, there was assembled (1618–1619) the famous Council of Dort, "a Council which has no parallel in the history of Protestantism."

The Dort Council was meant to be a general council of all the Calvinist churches to sit in judgment on Arminianism. The great majority of the representatives were Calvinists. Present were 84 theologians and 18 secular commissioners. Civil governments sent delegates to represent their countries. Deputies were present from Switzerland, Nassau, Hesse, Bremen, Scotland, and England. The Council met in 154 formal sessions from November 1618 to

---

[7] *History of Interpretation*, Farrar, F. W., p. 343.

May 1619. Arminius died before this Council was held.

The Arminians were summoned before this Council and given a hearing, but biased from the start, the Council's decision was a foregone conclusion. The old prejudice and jealousy was fanned into hotter flames. The Arminian doctrine of conditional predestination was examined and condemned. Arminius was branded a heretic. Two hundred Arminian pastors were deprived of their pastorates, and those who refused to be silenced were banished from their country.

The Council members were determined to crush the Arminian heresy. Arminian leaders were imprisoned. One was beheaded on the false charge of high treason. It was dangerous to oppose Calvinism, as Servetus, another theologian, learned when Calvin and his associates at Geneva burned him at the stake as a heretic.

The Dort Council did not settle anything about the 1300-year-old dispute, as many of the important church councils from the Council of Nice (324 A.D.) to the Council of Trent (1545–1563) also failed to settle doctrinal questions brought before them. Much of this history is a sad record of dishonorable intrigue, power politics, word jugglery, and evasion of facts. The Calvinists at Dort did not answer the difficulties and objections that beset their doctrines, nor have they to this day. What did "predestination" mean? In these councils, attempts to get Scriptural definitions never ceased.

Professor Emil Brunner of Zurich is generally considered one of the world's leading theologians in our day, and he once said that the best thing Christianity could do for the world would be to "give it a dictionary of Biblical terms." Anyone who knows the doctrinal history of predestination may agree.

Later, I shall give you the Biblical definitions for predestination and kindred terms, and the authoritative sources for them.

The above historical sketch of the predestination controversy should give you an idea of what it was all about. It is not necessary to take you through the long history of this complicated mass of confusion. I shall give you a few quotations from recent Calvinist writers and then we shall begin with our Scriptural proofs for conditional salvation.

Some Calvinists claim that we do not fairly present the Augustinian-Calvinist doctrine of predestination, so I have selected two recent popular full-fledged Calvinist writers who claim to be true exponents of Calvin's doctrine.

I quote first from the well-known and able Calvinist writer, Arthur W. Pink. He wrote in his *The Sovereignty of God*:

> God does not love everybody; if He did, He would love the devil. (p. 30) . . . It is God Himself who maketh the difference between the elect and the non-elect. (p. 61) . . . Faith is God's gift, and apart from this gift none would believe. The *cause* of His choice then lies within Himself and not in the objects of His choice. He chose the ones He did simply because He chose to choose them. (p. 71, his italic)

> The new birth is solely the work of God the Spirit and man has no part in it. This from the very nature of the case. Birth altogether excludes the idea of any effort or work on the part of the one who is born. Personally we have no more to do with our spiritual birth than we had with our natural birth. (p. 88)

> Again, faith is God's gift, and the purpose to give it only to some, involves the purpose *not* to give it to others. Without faith there is no salvation— "He that believeth not shall be damned"—hence if there were some of Adam's descendants to whom

He purposed not to give faith, it must be because
He ordained that *they* should be damned. (p. 101,
his italics)

He (God) fits the non-elect unto destruction by
His fore-ordinating decrees. Should it be asked
why God does this, the answer must be: To pro-
mote His own glory, i.e. the glory of His justice,
power and wrath. (p. 118)

On page 119, Mr. Pink quotes Calvin:

There are vessels prepared for destruction, that
is, given up and appointed to destruction; they are
also vessels of wrath, that is, *made and formed
for this end,* that they may be examples of God's
vengeance and displeasure. (his emphasis)

The next quotations come from *Shall Never Perish*: [8]

No man ever willed to be born into the human
race, and equally impotent is he to will to separate
himself from the human race.... As it is impossible for man, by free action, to separate himself
from the human race, so it is equally impossible
for him, by a free act, to separate himself from
God's kingdom. (pp. 119–120)

Truly, once a son of mankind, always a son of
mankind, and equally true, once a child of God,
always a child of God. There is no possibility for
a man, by his own will or action, to change
either of these conditions...all who are saved are
secure for all eternity. (p. 120)

When one has of his own free will accepted
Christ...he is given a new nature which makes
it impossible for him to will to return to his
former state. (p. 124)

We are not governed by reason but by revelation. (p. 129)

It is taught in Eph. 1:13–14, that after a person
has believed (a finished act) he is sealed with

[8] Strombeck, J. F., Van Kampen Press, 1948.

the Holy Spirit until the redemption of the pur-
chased possession. This passage once and for all
rules out the argument that one must continue
to believe. There is no need for continuous faith
on the part of the saved person. . . . (pp. 130–
131)

There are similar statements scattered throughout the books of Pink, Strombeck, and other Calvinist writers. It is fair to say that many Calvinists do
not agree with much that these authors have written
about predestination. One Calvinist minister recently
told me he wasn't sure what he believed about predestination. So the issue is clearly before us:

Is it true that sinners are damned without freedom of will or choice?

Is it true that the predestinated ones are "saved
without regard to what they may or may not do"?

Is it true that "if they sin, yet God so preserves
His Holy Spirit in them that they can never fall entirely out of the state of grace"?

Does the Bible teach that "the unchangeableness
of the divine decree excludes the possibility that they
should entirely fall away or be lost"?

Is salvation conditional or unconditional?

In our study, let us not be Calvinists nor Arminians but truth-seekers who accept nothing but
proved facts. Paul said: "Prove all things," and this
includes Bible doctrines. So let us accept only what
is proved. The world's foremost authorities on *Evidence* say: "What are the facts?" "Get the facts."
We shall try to get the facts—from Genesis to Revelation.

Our premise is this: Jesus said, "Salvation is of
the Jews." It was of the Jews because it was founded
on Jewish covenants. These covenants were conditional. Therefore, salvation is conditional. "Ye are
saved . . . *If ye continue.*"

3

Salvation Conditional
from the Beginning

GOD'S IF-CONDITION FOR CAIN AND ABEL

And in process of time it came to pass, that Cain brought of the fruit of the ground an offering unto the Lord.

And Abel, he also brought of the firstlings of his flock and of the fat thereof. And the Lord had respect unto Abel and to his offering:

But unto Cain and to his offering he had not respect. And Cain was very wroth, and his countenance fell.

And the Lord said unto Cain, Why art thou wroth? and why is thy countenance fallen?

If thou doest well, shalt thou not be accepted? and *if* thou doest not well, sin lieth at the door. And unto thee shall be his desire, and thou shalt rule over him. (Gen. 4: 3–7)

THIS STORY SHOULD BE SUFFICIENT to convince an unprejudiced mind that acceptance with God is conditional. Here God clearly stated His if-condition to Cain.

Cain's offering, the "fruit of the ground," was rejected by God. Abel's offering, the "firstlings of his flock and of the fat thereof," was accepted. When God "had respect" unto Abel and his offering, but did not have respect unto Cain and his offering, Cain became angry and his countenance fell.

God tried to reason with angry Cain, that He did not have an unconditional preference for Abel. God's acceptance of Abel was because of his "more excellent sacrifice" (Heb. 11:4). Cain *could* have done as Abel did, and if he would have satisfied the conditional requirement for offerings, he would have been accepted.

The Apostle John wrote:

> Not as Cain, who was of that wicked one, and slew his brother. And *wherefore slew he him?* Because his own *works* were evil, and his brother's righteous. (I John 3:12)

The Apostle here told us *why* Cain killed Abel. Cain was of "that wicked one." Cain's *works* were evil, but Abel's works were righteous. Cain's offering exhibited evil works. Abel's offering exhibited faith works. The world's first murder was caused by the hatred of evil worship for righteous worship. Cain's unbelief was revealed in his evil "works." Abel's faith was revealed in his righteous works.

Cain, the world's first apostate, rejected God's "if." Evil Cain worshipped God but not "by faith," as Abel did. All the world's religion today, as always, is divided into unbelief-worship and faith-worship. Abel's offering satisfied God's "if," Cain's did not. That is the whole story. The faith and worth of Abel's offering pleased God; the unbelief and cheapness of Cain's offering did not.

> By faith Abel offered unto God a more excellent sacrifice than Cain, *by which* he obtained witness that he was righteous, God testifying of his gifts. (Heb. 11:4)

God testified to Abel's "gifts," and it was his faith-gifts that God bore witness to. The faith-gifts was the fact on which the witness was based. "Faith without works is dead" (James 2: 20). "They profess that they know God; but in works they deny him" (Titus 1: 16).

The Cain spirit of worship continues to our day. Jude said, "Woe unto them! for they have gone in the *way* of Cain" (v. 11).

The "way of Cain" is a *system* of religion. It can always be identified and marked by the fact that it has no part with God's if-condition for acceptable worship. It is Cain-worship—and it hates Abel-like worship. "He that was born after the flesh persecuted him that was born after the Spirit, *even so it is now*" (Gal. 4: 29). As Cain rejected God's if-condition so also the Way-of-Cain religion rejects it today. Beware of any religion that rejects God's "if."

With these facts before us, can the reader agree with the Calvinist writers here quoted? "Those who are saved are not saved because of their faith or repentance or any other reason." "The calling of God then is the carrying out of His own purpose independent of the saved one's works."

If Abel had offered the same kind of sacrifice as Cain, would he have been declared "righteous" by God?

Would Cain have been rejected if he had obeyed God's "if" and had offered faith-gifts, like Abel?

Is not a man righteous if his "works" are righteous? And is he not evil if his works are evil?

Is not the same if-condition for acceptable worship required of us as for Cain and Abel?

4

Salvation Conditional in the Abrahamic Covenant

> In the same day the Lord made a covenant with Abram. (Gen. 15:18)
>
> As for me, behold, my covenant is with thee. (Gen. 17:4)
>
> And I will establish my covenant between me and thee and thy seed after thee in their generations. (Gen. 17:7)

IT WILL BE HELPFUL IF WE FIRST KNOW what an ancient covenant was. The Hebrew word for covenant is *berith*, and the Greek word is *diatheke*. The definition of covenant in Hebrew and Greek is: "will" — "purpose" — "disposition."

The reader can check this definition of covenant in some of the leading lexicons.[1]

---

[1] *A Greek-English Lexicon of the New Testament*, Arndt & Gingrich, p. 182. University of Chicago Press, 1957.

Thayer's Greek-English Lexicon of the New Testament, p. 136. 1889.

Expository Dictionary of New Testament Words, Vine, W. E., V. I, p. 250. Oliphants, Ltd., London, 1948.

Vocabulary of the Greek New Testament, Moulton & Milligan, p. 148. Eerdmans, 1959.

Synonyms of the Old Testament, Girdlestone, R. B., p. 214. Eerdmans.

Student's Hebrew Lexicon, Davies & Mitchell, p. 105. Kregel, 1957.

A Bible covenant was God's declaration of His "will-purpose-disposition" toward those with whom He entered into covenant. In making His gracious proposals to men, God, the Covenantor, expressed His will and purpose to His people, the covenantees. He pledged himself that something is done, or would be done, for the covenantees upon the performance by the covenantees of such conditions as stated in the covenant. We shall see many proofs as we proceed to show that God's covenants were conditional.

There is much nonsense taught in theology with the phrase, "Sovereign will of God." The Eternal Security teachers use it often. And some of them use it without explaining what they mean by it. The Bible does not use it. It is a term invented by men and loaded with a meaning about predestination that the Bible does not bear. Other doctrines are also taught by other teachers with words and terms that the Bible does not use.

God's covenant with Abraham imposed a severe condition from the beginning.

> Now the Lord had said unto Abram, Get thee out of thy country, and from thy kindred, and from thy father's house, unto a land that I will shew thee.... So Abram departed, as the Lord had spoken unto him. (Gen. 12: 1–4)

The history of Israel begins with Abraham. In Scripture he is called the "father" of the Jewish people. Proud Jews claimed that they were Abraham's children (Matt. 3: 9). All God's dealings with Israel—past, present, and future—are founded in the Abrahamic Covenant. Salvation is based on the Abrahamic Covenant—and this was a *conditional* covenant.

Other Bible covenants also have their foundation in the Abrahamic Covenant. The Abrahamic Covenant is embodied in, and is carried through, each succeeding covenant. The New Covenant is based on the Abrahamic Covenant. God's eternal purpose of salvation was conceived "before the foundation of the world" (Matt. 25: 34; Eph. 1: 4), but this purpose is accomplished through the Abrahamic Covenant. Our Saviour was "slain before the foundation of the world" (Rev. 13: 8); but the Saviour said, "Salvation is of the Jews" (John 4: 22).

Paul stressed the fact that Christ is the Seed of Abraham (Gal. 3: 16). The Abrahamic Covenant is the basis of many Messianic prophecies. All redemption is based on the Abrahamic Covenant, although conceived before the foundation of the world. And it began with God's *call* to Abraham.

> By faith Abraham, when he was *called* to go out into a place which he should after receive for an inheritance, obeyed; and he went out, not knowing whither he went. (Heb. 11: 8)

This was the first condition of the Abrahamic Covenant. And anyone able to recognize a fact when he sees it cannot deny that it was a condition. What God promised to do for Abraham was conditional upon his leaving his country, home, and kindred. He had to forsake all who would not go with him. If Abraham had not "obeyed" this condition, probably we would never have heard of him.

Doubtless Abraham was fondly attached to his native home, and it may not have been easy for him to forsake the family ties and cherished affections. But "by faith" he left all and went out to a life of testing as God's covenant-partner. He was a wanderer in the earth, living in tents in a "strange country" (Heb. 11: 9).

Had he "been mindful of that country" he left, he could have returned (Heb. 11: 15). There was no constraint, no coercion. Abraham acted with his own free will and choice. He obeyed God's call, and it is nonsense to speak of obedience without free choice.

It should be evident even to the casual reader that God's predestinating purpose in Abraham's life was related to, and conditional upon, a call to separation and obedience that required the acting of faith. Predestination does not stand alone in the Scriptures. It is related to, and is conditional upon, other truths. Here are a few examples:

> Moreover whom he did predestinate, them he also called: and whom he called, them he also justified: and whom he justified, them he also glorified. (Rom. 8: 30)

This is the way it was with Abraham. His calling and justification were part of God's predestinating purpose. Between Abraham's predestination and glorification, he was "called" and "justified." God, in predestinating Abraham's glorification, also predestinated the *means* for this. The Apostles gave much emphasis to this fact of God's *call.*

We are "called to be saints" (I Cor. 1: 2). "God hath . . . called us . . . unto holiness" (I Thess. 4: 7). We are "called" to "fight the good fight of faith"— "called" to "lay hold on eternal life" (I Tim. 6: 12). God has "called us with an holy calling" (II Tim. 1: 9). "But as he which hath called you is holy, so be ye holy" (I Pet. 1: 15). These and other texts give strong support to the fact that predestination does not stand alone in the Scriptures.

In the writings of the Eternal Security teachers, you will not find predestination used in relation to these conditional subjects. They would destroy their case for unconditional salvation if they did. In disconnecting predestination from these truths, they are guilty of a dangerous distortion of God's Word. And if we used the same method of interpretation on other doctrines, we could destroy the meaning of other important Bible truths. Some of the most dangerous errors in Christianity today are the results of this method of interpretation.

God called Abraham to forsake all. And Jesus said,

> Whosoever he be of you that forsaketh not all that he hath, he cannot be my disciple. (Luke 14:33)

This forsaking all is the acting of faith. It is the work of faith, not the "works of the law." Salvation is God's grace and love and mercy to sinful mankind. It is not for man to boast or glory in the works of his faith. The acts of his faith are the fulfilling of God's conditions for salvation. Abraham, by his faith, fulfilled the conditions of God's calling in his life, and Paul said that all who have faith will also "walk in the steps of that faith of our father Abraham" (Rom. 4:12). The forsake-all condition was clearly stated by Jesus as a requirement to be His disciple.

We now consider the second condition in the Abrahamic Covenant.

> I am the Almighty God; walk before me, and be thou perfect.
>
> And I will make my covenant between me and thee, and will multiply thee exceedingly.
>
> And Abram fell on his face: and God talked with him, saying,
>
> As for me, behold, my covenant is with thee, and thou shalt be a father of many nations. (Gen. 17:1-4)

The first condition required that Abraham leave his country and kindred. The second condition commanded him to "walk" (continually) before God. He left Chaldea by faith, and by a continual act of faith, he satisfied the covenant condition of a continual walk before God. Men talk much about the sovereign will of God in relation to salvation, but divine sovereignty imposed these covenant conditions upon Abraham. Not to have obeyed these conditions would have been disobedience, unbelief, and an offense to divine sovereignty.

New Covenant law has the same moral conditions as the Abrahamic Covenant. We must "walk in the steps of that faith of our father Abraham." This truth has frequent emphasis in the New Covenant.

In Romans 6:4, we "walk in newness of life." In Luke 1:6, God's covenant members walk "in all the commandments and ordinances of the Lord blameless." In John 12:35, the New Covenantor commanded: "Walk while ye have the light, lest darkness come upon you." Our only security and protection against darkness is to walk in the light.

In Galatians 6:16, Paul gave his blessing to those who "walk according to this rule" of New Testament righteousness. In Ephesians 5:2, 8, we are commanded by the New Covenant apostle to "walk in love" and to "walk as children of light." Colossians 1:10 tells us to "walk worthy of the Lord unto all pleasing." From Galatians 5:16, we are told we must "walk in the Spirit." I John 1:6 says that those who profess to be saved and "walk in darkness" are liars. I John 2:6 declares: He who is saved "ought himself also to walk, *even as he walked.*" III John 4 says that the true children of God "walk in truth." Those who are not of the truth walk in "lusts" (I Pet. 4:3). Paul gave us a *test* by which we can determine who is of God and who is not. He said we are to "mark them which walk," and if they walk according to the "ensample" Paul gave us, then they obey the New Covenant conditions and are saved (Phil. 3:17). Those who fail the walk-test are not saved.

Is not the New Covenant opposed to the teaching that our salvation does not depend on "anything that we may or may not do"?

In Genesis 17:9–14, the Covenantor added the third condition to the Abrahamic Covenant:

> And God said unto Abraham, *Thou* shalt keep my covenant therefore, thou, and thy seed after thee in their generations.

> This is my covenant, which ye shall keep, between me and you and thy seed after thee; Every man child among you shall be circumcised.

> And ye shall circumcise the flesh of your foreskin; and it shall be a token of the covenant betwixt me and you....

> He that is born in thy house, and he that is bought with thy money, must needs be circumcised: and my covenant shall be in your flesh for an everlasting covenant. And the uncircumcised man child whose flesh of his foreskin is not circumcised, that soul shall be *cut off* from his people; he hath *broken my covenant.*

Abraham and his family were placed under this covenant condition. Those who did not obey the condition were "cut off" from the covenant. Covenant-breakers were not allowed to remain in the covenant family. God told Abraham in verse 4: "As for me, behold, my covenant is with thee. . . ." The *Pulpit Commentary* comments on this: "*As for me,* is equivalent to 'so far as I am concerned,' or 'I, for my part.' "

God had His part in the covenant, and Abraham and his family had their parts. God offered His covenant to men, and for His part, as far as He was concerned, it was done. God recognizes His oath-bound covenant responsibilities to perform and make good His promises. The Covenantor fixed the conditions and pledged himself to His covenantees. If the covenantees broke the covenant conditions, they were cut off from the covenant. They forfeited their covenant rights.

Abraham lived by faith and obedience to the covenant conditions. God required that he "keep" the covenant, and no one could remain in the covenant who did not likewise keep its conditions. There was no such security as *once in the covenant, always in the covenant.*

In the Old Testament covenants the death penalty was often inflicted for covenant violations. We shall see more of this in the Sinai Covenant. We look now at the fourth condition in the Abrahamic Covenant.

> And it came to pass after these things, that God did tempt [test] Abraham, and said unto him, Abraham: and he said, Behold, here I am.
>
> And he said, Take now thy son, thine only son Isaac, whom thou lovest, and get thee into the land of Moriah; and offer him there for a burnt offering upon one of the mountains which I will tell thee of.
>
> And Abraham stretched forth his hand, and took the knife to slay his son.
>
> And the angel of the Lord called unto him out of heaven, and said, Abraham, Abraham: and he said, Here am I.
>
> And he said, Lay not thine hand upon the lad, neither do thou any thing unto him: for now I know that thou fearest God, seeing thou hast not withheld thy son, thine only son from me. (Gen. 22:1, 2, 10–12)

This was doubtless the greatest test of Abraham's life. It was *Abraham* who was tested. Some teachers deny free will and liberty of choice, and say it is all sovereign will. But if Abraham was not tested with his free will and choice, then, *what* was it that was tested that day on Moriah's mount? Surely, God

was not testing His own sovereign will. Observe
what God said about Abraham after the test:

> By myself have I sworn, saith the Lord, for *be-
> cause thou hast done this thing,* and hast not
> withheld thy son, thine only son:

> That in blessing I will bless thee, and in multiply-
> ing I will multiply thy seed as the stars of the
> heaven, and as the sand which is upon the sea
> shore; and thy seed shall possess the gate of
> his enemies;

> And in thy seed shall all the nations of the earth
> be blessed; *because thou hast obeyed my voice.*
> (Gen. 22: 16–18)

Now, dear reader, with these facts before us, I
ask you a fair question: When God said, "because
thou hast done this thing . . . because thou hast
obeyed my voice," by all the laws of language and
logic, does this not prove that God's covenant dealings with Abraham were *conditional?* Would God
have made the promises to Abraham if he had not
obeyed these conditions?

Consider another fact. When God told Isaac to
go down into Egypt, He said:

> Sojourn in this land, and I will be with thee, and
> will bless thee; for unto thee, and unto thy seed,
> I will give all these countries, and I will perform
> the oath which I sware unto Abraham thy father;

> And I will make thy seed to multiply as the stars
> of heaven, and will give unto thy seed all these
> countries; and in thy seed shall all the nations of
> the earth be blessed:

> Because that Abraham obeyed my voice, and kept
> my charge, my commandments, my statutes, and
> my laws. (Gen. 26: 3–5)

The *Jamieson, Fausset, Brown Commentary* is one
of the highly respected commentaries, and in their
exposition of the above Scripture, they present both

the divine and human parts of the Abrahamic Covenant:

> The Covenant securing these blessings originated entirely in Divine grace; but it was suspended on the condition that Abraham should walk before God...and since he had through the grace which had enabled him to attain an extraordinary strength of faith, fully met that condition by an obedience honored with the strongest expression of Divine approval, — Isaac, his son, was now assured that the covenant would progressively take effect....

God had foreknowledge of Abraham, but this foreknowledge did not make him a predestinated puppet. This foreknowledge did not dispense with the covenant conditions; it did not set aside the requirements for faith and obedience. The covenant fulfillments did not come to Abraham by God's foreknowledge without Abraham's fulfillment of the conditions.

Three times God connected the covenant fulfillments with—"Because thou hast *done* this thing ... because thou hast obeyed my voice." This is also indicated in Genesis 18:19, where God said He knew Abraham and what he would do:

> For I know him, that he will command his children and his household after him, and they shall keep the way of the Lord, to *do* justice and judgment; *that* the Lord may bring upon Abraham that which he hath spoken of him.

This text teaches that God chose Abraham to do His will and to carry out His purposes "that" the covenant blessings might come upon him. The Hebrew for "that" means, literally, "to the end that," "in order that" the blessings might come upon him. "His habitual attention to, and faithful performance of, these duties, was a compliance with the conditions on which the Divine promises had been made to him." [2]

Dr. S. R. Driver (1846–1914), Regius Professor of Hebrew at Oxford, was one of the revisers of the English translation of the Old Testament (1876–1884) and one of the top-ranking Old Testament authorities of modern times.

Professor Driver wrote concerning the condition of the Abrahamic Covenant in Genesis 17:1–4; he said: "Upon this condition . . . God grants His covenant" to Abraham. "Walk before me, and be thou blameless." "The condition Abraham is called upon to fulfill . . . [is] the duty of leading generally a righteous and holy life. . . . Upon this condition . . . God grants His covenant." On the command that Abraham offer up Isaac, Professor Driver said: "God tested Abraham to ascertain whether his faith . . . is real." [3]

When Jesus was teaching in Israel, His sharpest rebukes went to a group of hypocritical Jews called Pharisees. They boasted that Abraham was their father, and they considered themselves the predestinated heirs of Abraham's eternal kingdom. But Jesus exposed them with *one test*:

> They answered and said unto him, Abraham is our father. Jesus saith unto them, *If* ye were Abraham's children, ye would *do* the *works* of Abraham. (John 8:39)

Jesus, with this Abrahamic works-test, exposed them as being of "your father the devil" (v. 44). The true spiritual sons of Abraham will continually obey God's covenant conditions, as Abraham did.

---

[2] *Jamieson, Fausset, Brown Commentary.* (See also *Pulpit Commentary.*)

[3] *The Book Of Genesis,* Driver, S. R., pp. 185, 217; 3rd edition, 1904.

Abraham did not have a one-act-of-faith experience. Christ here made the New Covenant conditional by imposing similar conditions as those required of Abraham.

The New Covenant is founded on the Abrahamic Covenant. Salvation is of the Jews. Abraham is the "father of us all" (Rom. 4:16). The Abrahamic Covenant was for Abraham and "thy seed after thee in their generations." This covenant was not stripped of its conditions as it passed to Abraham's descendants. It was not conditional for Abraham and unconditional for his seed.

Not only salvation but the Kingdom of God is founded on the Abrahamic Covenant. And membership in the Kingdom is conditional. In my book on the Covenants,[4] I have given many Biblical proofs for the fact that the Kingdom of God is founded on the Abrahamic Covenant.

God gave Abraham an everlasting covenant and an everlasting kingdom "because" he obeyed God's covenant conditions. God also gives us an eternal covenant of life if we "do the works of Abraham." The Bible tells us more about Abraham's faith than about the faith of anyone. It is held up to our view as a model of faith. It was a faith that exhibited his works, and Jesus required the same works of faith from those who claimed salvation in New Testament times.

The works of Abraham were continual. From Chaldea, where he was called to forsake all, to Moriah's mount, where he was commanded to offer up his son Isaac, Abraham believed and obeyed.

God's covenants carry a guaranteed security. They are instruments of certainty. They are *Covenants of Surety*. But this divine suretyship is denied

---

[4] *God's Covenants and Our Time*, Duty, G., Bethany Fellowship, Inc., 1964.

to all who violate its conditions. So, it is not a question of *what* is in the covenant, but *who* is in it. Again, these covenants had no such security as *once in the covenant, always in the covenant,* unless one continued in the covenant.

The facts of the Abrahamic Covenant force us to the conclusion that God's covenant of salvation to Abraham was conditional. The leave-all condition, the walk-before-me condition, and the offer-up-Isaac condition place it beyond all reasonable doubt. Salvation is of the Jews. The Abrahamic Covenant is the foundation of Jewish salvation. The Abrahamic Covenant is conditional.

5

The If-Condition in the Sinaitic Covenant

THE SINAI COVENANT was based on the Abrahamic Covenant. It is a further development of the Abrahamic; and like the Abrahamic, it is a conditional covenant.

There are many "ifs" in this covenant that God made with Israel at Sinai. The if-condition appears frequently from Exodus to Deuteronomy. Israelites were called "Sons of the Covenant," but the covenant provided them with security only while they remained in the covenant and obeyed covenant laws.

The Jews always boasted of their natural covenant birthright, but Moses, the prophets, John Baptist, Jesus, and the Apostles repeatedly warned them about the false security of this deceptive assurance.

When Moses offered Israel God's covenant proposal, they were given time to ponder its terms. The covenant was read to them again the second day. They could accept or reject it. With their own free will they could say yes or no. Here's the covenant God offered them:

> In the third month...came they into the wilderness of Sinai....

And Moses went up unto God, and the Lord called unto him out of the mountain, saying, Thus shalt thou say to the house of Jacob, and tell the children of Israel:

Ye have seen what I did unto the Egyptians, and how I bare you on eagles' wings, and brought you unto myself.

Now therefore, *if* ye will obey my voice indeed, and *keep* my covenant, then ye shall be a peculiar treasure unto me above all people: for all the earth is mine:

And ye shall be unto me a kingdom of priests, and an holy nation.

And Moses took half of the blood, and put it in basins; and half of the blood he sprinkled on the altar.

And he took the book of the covenant, and read in the audience of the people: and they said, All that the Lord hath said will we do, and be obedient.

And Moses took the blood, and sprinkled it on the people, and said, Behold the blood of the covenant, which the Lord hath made with you concerning all these words. (Ex. 19:1–6; 24:6–8)

When Moses read to them the second time the "book of the covenant ... concerning all these words," the people said, "All that the Lord hath said will we do, and be obedient." They made no excuses about inability to obey it. They did not object that it was too strict. They said nothing about it as being unreasonable. When they freely accepted it, Moses performed the ceremony of ratification and the covenant blood was sprinkled upon them—which would not have been done without their acceptance of the covenant. The covenant bond was then "established" between God, the Covenantor, and Israel, the covenantees. God then became to them Jehovah Who Binds Himself.

God guaranteed all promises and provisions of the covenant subject to the if-condition. If the covenant was not realized to them, they had only themselves to blame. Only on condition of their full compliance to the "if" would Jehovah be their covenant God. If they obeyed the requirements, they had their "part and lot" in the covenant.

God said the covenant was "My covenant." Everything originates with God. All flows from His free grace and love. No praise to man for anything. He cannot *earn* or *merit* anything from God, not with all his obedience and faith. But the Covenantor required that, to enter into the blessings of His covenant, we must also enter into its conditions.

Various punishments were imposed upon covenant breakers. They were "cut off" from the covenant, and often the death penalty was inflicted upon the Sons of the Covenant. They were banished from the covenant and put to death. The covenant violator not only forfeited his covenant rights, but also forfeited his life. It was "a sin unto death" (I John 5:16).

There was no atonement for willful violations of Mosaic Covenant law. The violator had to "bear his iniquity" (Lev. 17:16); it would not be borne by the covenant sacrifices. God said, "I will set my face against that man, and will cut him off from among his people" (Lev. 20:2, 3). See Leviticus 20:17, 19, 27 for other sins that the covenant sacrifices could not atone for. The blood of the transgressors was upon their own heads.

The willful covenant violator could not say he was sorry and ask Moses for mercy. "He that despised Moses' law died without mercy under two or three witnesses" (Heb. 10:28). There was no pity from God, Moses, or Israel.

There were frequent threats of excommunication

and death in Moses' law. Here are a few of many: Leviticus 7:20, 21, 25, 27; 17:4, 9, 10, 14; 18:29; 19:8; 20:6, 10, 11, 13, 18; 23:29. God said, "Whosoever hath sinned against me him will I blot out of my book" (Ex. 32:33). And Jesus said, "He that overcometh, the same shall be clothed in white raiment; and I will not blot out his name out of the book of life, but I will confess his name before my Father, and before his angels" (Rev. 3:5). And Paul, in the New Covenant, speaking about the world's sin against God's laws, said: "They which commit such things are *worthy of death*" (Rom. 1:32). And Hebrews 10:26, 27 says:

> For if we sin wilfully after that we have received the knowledge of the truth, there remaineth no more sacrifice for sins,
>
> But a certain fearful looking for of judgment and fiery indignation which shall devour the adversaries.

The Covenantor often referred to His covenant, and often held that all-important "if" before His covenantees:

> *If* ye walk in my statutes, and keep my commandments, and *do* them. . . . I will have respect unto you. . .and establish my covenant among you. . . .
>
> But *if* ye will not hearken unto me, and will not do all these commandments;. . .and *if* ye shall despise my statutes, or *if* your soul abhor my judgments. . . . And *if* ye walk contrary unto me. . . and *if* ye will not be reformed by me by these things,. . .then will I also walk contrary unto you. . .and I will set my face against you, and ye shall be slain before your enemies. (Lev. 26:3–28)
>
> *If* they shall confess their iniquity. . .*if* then their uncircumcised hearts be humbled, and they then accept of the punishment of their iniquity:
>
> *Then* will I remember my covenant with Jacob, and also my covenant with Isaac, and also my

covenant with Abraham will I remember; and I
will remember the land. (Lev. 26:40–42)

God always had a faithful remnant through
whom He fulfilled His obligations to Abraham. They
were covenant-keepers.

God never ceased to warn Israel of the dangers
of breaking His covenant. See Numbers 9:13; 15:30;
19:13. Moses, in his farewell messages to Israel,
warned them of the covenant commandments, and
told them that everything depended upon their obedience. Perhaps they wearied of the repetition.

> I call heaven and earth to witness against you
> this day, that ye shall soon utterly perish from
> off the land whereunto ye go over to possess it;
> ye shall not prolong your days upon it; but shall
> utterly be destroyed. . . . But *if* from thence thou
> shalt seek the Lord thy God, thou shalt find him,
> *if* thou seek him with all thy heart and with all
> thy soul. (Deut. 4:26–29)

Moses, before going to his death, continued the
repetition:

> Behold, I set before you this day a blessing and a
> curse;
>
> A blessing *if* ye obey the commandments of the
> Lord your God, which I command you this day:
>
> And a curse *if* ye will not obey the command-
> ments of the Lord your God. (Deut. 11:26–28)

Scattered frequently throughout Moses' final appeal to Israel, the great law-giver warned them again
and again with that "if." Check the following references and see how this was pressing on the mind
of Moses who, after these warnings, left them to go
to his death: Deuteronomy 8:19, 20; 11:22; 19:9.
And in chapter 15:5, he said God would honor His
covenant with them "only *if* thou carefully hearken
unto the voice of the Lord thy God . . . to do all these
commandments."

In Deuteronomy 27:15–26, Moses listed 12 curses that would come upon them for *breach of covenant.* There were covenant blessings and covenant curses. And when the curses came upon them, Moses said other nations would say:

> Wherefore hath the Lord done thus unto this land? what meaneth the heat of this great anger?
>
> Then men shall say, Because they have forsaken the covenant of the Lord God of their fathers. (Deut. 29:24, 25)

When Moses drew near the end of his mighty appeal to the covenant people, still warning and threatening, he said,

> But *if* thine heart turn away, so that thou wilt not hear, but shalt be drawn away, and worship other gods, and serve them:
>
> I denounce unto you this day, that ye shall surely perish, and that ye shall not prolong your days upon the land. (Deut. 30:17, 18)

Then Moses, with prophetic discernment, told them:

> For I know thy rebellion, and thy stiff neck; behold, while I am yet alive with you this day, ye have been rebellious against the Lord; and how much more after my death?
>
> For I know that after my death ye will utterly corrupt yourselves, and turn aside from the way which I have commanded you; and evil will befall you in the latter days; because ye will do evil in the sight of the Lord. (Deut. 31:27, 29)

The *Pulpit Commentary* in its exposition of Exodus 19:1–15 comments on this Sinai Covenant:

> The condition of the fulfilment of promise is that the people obey God's covenant voice, and keep his covenant. On no other terms could God consent to be their God, and on no other terms would he consent to have them for his people.

In all God's dealing with us *he has respect to
our liberty.* The condition here is a *believing obedience.* The Hebrew word for "obey" seems to
carry pregnantly within all its meanings—hearing,
listening, heeding, trusting, acting according to
what we hear and believe. (their emphasis)

I have not quoted all the if-references in the
Pentateuch because it would have been needless
repetition, but we may note in passing that the if-
emphasis was continued by Joshua:

If ye forsake the Lord, and serve strange gods,
then he will turn and do you hurt, and consume
you after that he hath done you good. (Josh.
24: 20)

Suppose we had not another Scripture to prove
our case for conditional salvation, would not those
we have seen thus far be sufficient to prove our
case? Is not Israel's horrible 3000-year history of
persecution and slaughter abundant evidence to any
fair-minded interpreter that the Jewish covenants
were *conditional?*

There has been a question among interpreters
whether this "if" has the same conditional meaning
in the Hebrew text as in the English Bible. So, I
quote Hebrew scholars who hold high positions of
authority.

On the if-condition in the Sinaitic Covenant, Keil
and Delitzsch wrote in their *Biblical Commentary on
the Old Testament*: [1]

The theocracy [was] established by the conclusion of the covenant...the maintenance of this
covenant was the indispensable subjective condition.

This promise of Jehovah expressed the design of
the call of Israel, to which it was to be fully
conducted by the covenant institution of the the-

---

[1] V. 2, p. 97, V. 3, p. 454. Eerdmans, 1949.

ocracy, if it maintained the covenant with Jehovah.

[The "if" of Deut. 30:10 was] A renewed enforcement of the indispensable condition of salvation.

R. B. Girdlestone, another top Hebrew authority, wrote concerning the conditions of the Old Testament covenants: [2]

If Israel followed the course of obedience, certain happy consequences would ensue. If they disobeyed, various specified evil would follow. So it was in the case of individuals. Jeremiah said to Zedekiah, "If thou wilt go forth to the king of Babylon's princes, then thy soul shall live... but if thou wilt not go...thou shalt not escape out of their hand." (Jer. 38:17, 18)

Violators of Mosaic covenant law were excluded from the covenant-camp until they were declared clean and the required sacrifice was offered for them. God's covenant sanctuary was not allowed to be defiled even by unintentional sins (Lev. 5:15–19). No Israelite could continue in sin and continue in God's covenant of salvation for Israel. God set His face against the transgressor and excluded him from the covenant (Lev. 20:3). There was salvation under the canopy of Jehovah's covenant protection, but the Israelites had to remain where this salvation was. They had to move with it and live with it. Their lives were sustained and saved only as they continued in the covenant life.

One act of faith could not save the Jews under Moses. After their deliverance from Egypt, their continued covenant obedience was demanded. Covenant protection was withdrawn from those who did not obey and they died unsaved.

2 *The Grammar of Prophecy*, Girdlestone, R. B., p. 25, Kregel, 1955.

All redemption is placed on a covenant basis. This basis is the Jewish covenants. But there was no such security in these covenants as "once in the covenant, always in the covenant."

Salvation is of the Jews. The Sinaitic Covenant was of the Jews, and the evidence gives strong support to our conclusion that this covenant was conditional.

6

The If-Condition in the

Davidic Covenant

THE ABRAHAMIC COVENANT is the foundation of the Davidic Covenant. It is also the foundation of the New Covenant (Luke 1:72; Acts 3:25; Gal. 3:16). The blessings and conditions of the Abrahamic Covenant were continued through succeeding generations because this covenant was made to Abraham and to "thy seed after thee in *their generations* for an everlasting covenant" (Gen. 17:7). It was conditional to Abraham and conditional for his seed.

It may interest you to know how the Davidic Covenant originated. God takes the initiative but He always needs something to initiate with. Some teachers tell us there are mysteries in these covenants that human minds cannot penetrate, but the Bible certainly reveals the *reasons* for them. God not only tells us *what,* He tells us *why.* As we saw how the Abrahamic Covenant originated with Abraham's obedience to God's call, so we shall learn how the Davidic Covenant began.

When King Saul had persistently disobeyed the commandments of the Lord, God told the prophet Samuel:

> It repenteth me that I have set up Saul to be king:
> for he is turned back from following me, and hath
> not performed my commandments. And it grieved
> Samuel: and he cried unto the Lord all night.
> (I Sam. 15: 11)

Samuel delivered God's message to the unfaithful king, and said:

> Behold, to obey is better than sacrifice, and to
> hearken than the fat of rams.
>
> For rebellion is as the sin of witchcraft, and stub-
> bornness is as iniquity and idolatry. *Because* thou
> hast rejected the word of the Lord, he hath also
> rejected thee from being king.
>
> And Saul said unto Samuel, I have sinned: for I
> have transgressed the commandment of the Lord.
> ...Now therefore, I pray thee, pardon my sin,
> and turn again with me, that I may worship the
> Lord.
>
> And Samuel said unto Saul, I will not return with
> thee: for thou hast rejected the word of the Lord,
> and the Lord hath rejected thee from being king
> over Israel. (I Sam. 15: 22–26)

Now, if the facts of language can prove anything, this language forcefully reveals God's reason for Saul's rejection as Israel's king. Saul's *rebellion* against God's commandments was as the "sin of witchcraft . . . and idolatry." The same satanic spirit that works in witchcraft and idolatry also works in those who rebel against and disobey God's commandments. There was no excuse here for "inherent weakness," or "compulsive complex," or anything else. Modern religious psychology could learn a great lesson here. Samuel also told Saul:

> Thou hast done foolishly: thou hast not kept the
> commandment of the Lord thy God, which he
> commanded thee: for now would the Lord have
> established thy kingdom upon Israel for ever.

> But now thy kingdom shall not continue: the Lord
> hath sought him a man after his own heart, and
> the Lord hath commanded him to be captain over
> his people, *because* thou hast not kept that which
> the Lord commanded thee. (I Sam. 13:13, 14)

Samuel repeated God's reason's for Saul's rejection. There was no mysterious predestination in the reasons. Saul was rejected and dethroned "because" he failed to obey the covenant commandments. Samuel told him God would have "established thy kingdom upon Israel forever" if he had obeyed. God doesn't play favorites. He has wise reasons for His choices. "But now thy kingdom shall not continue: the Lord hath sought him a man after his own heart." David was chosen to fulfill the conditions that Saul failed to keep. God would have done the same for Saul that He did for David if he had not been disobedient. Paul, in Acts 13:22, referred to Saul's rejection and David's selection:

> And when he had removed him, he raised up unto
> them David to be their king; to whom also he gave
> testimony, and said, I have found David the son
> of Jesse, a man after mine own heart, *which
> shall fulfil all my will.*

David, like Abraham, possessed remarkable spiritual qualities. Not only did he desire to do God's will but he had intense thirstings for God. "As the hart panteth after the waterbrooks, so panteth my soul after thee, O God." "My soul thirsteth for God, for the living God." "My soul followeth hard after thee" (Ps. 42:1, 2; 63:8). With these facts before us, who cannot see that the Davidic Covenant had a *conditional* basis?

Eternal Security teachers use the term "sovereign will" when speaking of God's predestinating purpose. But when God was looking for a man to be His king over Israel, He was searching for a man who would obey the commands of that sovereign will. The search ended when He found David.

Christ was born to Israel to accomplish promises made to Abraham and David. He was the seed of Abraham and the seed of David (Gal. 3:16; Rom. 1:3). Salvation is of the Jews, but this salvation came as a result of promises given to men who had obeyed the conditions of covenants made to them. Therefore, the fulfillment of these covenants could not be *unconditional* when the original covenants were *conditional*.

From Cain and Abel, to the Abrahamic Covenant, to the Sinaitic Covenant, to the Davidic Covenant, repetition of the if-condition in the covenants never ceased. The prophets gave it continual emphasis. Samuel continued the pressure:

> And Samuel spake unto all the house of Israel, saying, *If* ye do return unto the Lord with all your hearts, then put away the strange gods... from among you, and prepare your hearts unto the Lord, and serve him only: and he will deliver you....
>
> *If* ye will fear the Lord, and serve him, and obey his voice, and not rebel against the commandment of the Lord, then shall both ye and also the king that reigneth over you *continue* following the Lord your God:
>
> But *if* ye will not obey the voice of the Lord, but rebel against the commandment of the Lord, then shall the hand of the Lord be against you, as it was against your fathers. (I Sam. 7:3; 12: 14, 15)

Samuel made everything depend upon their continual covenant obedience. He would not have accepted a one-act-of-faith from them. He specified that they must "continue" to follow the Lord. If they continued to keep the covenant, then Jehovah was ready to go into action for them against their enemies. Jehovah was Israel's War-God.

David understood that the covenant God gave him was conditional. He stressed this fact to Solomon upon his accession to the throne. David gave him God's message about his reign:

> Solomon thy son, he shall build my house and my courts: for I have chosen him to be my son, and I will be his father.
>
> Moreover I will establish his kingdom forever, *if* he be constant to do my commandments and my judgments, as at this day.
>
> Now therefore in the sight of all Israel...and in the audience of our God, keep and seek for all the commandments of the Lord your God....
>
> And thou, Solomon my son, know thou the God of thy father, and serve him with a perfect heart and with a willing mind...*if* thou seek him, he will be found of thee; but *if* thou forsake him, *he will cast thee off forever.* (I Chron. 28:6-9)

When Solomon had built his temple, God made this covenant with him:

> Concerning this house which thou art in building, *if* thou wilt walk in my statutes, and execute my judgments, and keep all my commandments to walk in them; then will I perform my word with thee, which I spake unto David thy father. (I Kings 6:12)
>
> The Lord appeared to Solomon the second time. ...And the Lord said unto him, I have heard thy prayer and thy supplication, that thou hast made before me.... And *if* thou wilt walk before me as David thy father walked, in integrity of heart, and in uprightness, to do according to all that I have commanded thee, and wilt keep my statutes and my judgments:
>
> Then I will establish the throne of thy kingdom upon Israel for ever, as I promised to David thy father....

> But *if* ye shall at all turn from following me, ye
> or your children, and will not keep my command-
> ments and my statutes which I have set before
> you...: then will I cut off Israel out of the land
> which I have given them...and Israel shall be a
> proverb and a byword among all people:

> And at this house, which is high, every one that
> passeth by it shall be astonished, and shall hiss;
> and they shall say, Why hath the Lord done thus
> unto this land, and to this house?

> And they shall answer, Because they forsook the
> Lord their God. (I Kings 9:2–9)

Solomon understood that God's covenant with
him was conditional. At the dedication of his magnificent temple, Solomon offered his prayer to the
"Lord God of Israel...who keepest covenant and
mercy with thy servants that walk before thee with
all their heart." He prayed for God's blessings upon
the nation "if" the people obeyed the covenant conditions (I Kings 8:1–61).

When Solomon broke covenant with God and
went into idolatrous sin, God executed His threat
against him for his apostasy. God told him:

> Forasmuch as this is done of thee, and thou hast
> not kept my covenant and my statutes, which I
> have commanded thee, I will surely rend the
> kingdom from thee.... Howbeit I will not rend
> away all the kingdom; but will give one tribe to
> thy son for David my servant's sake. (I Kings
> 11:11–13)

Now here is a passage from II Samuel 7:12–16
from which Eternal Security teachers argue that the
Davidic Covenant was unconditional. God told
David:

> And when thy days be fulfilled, and thou shalt
> sleep with thy fathers, I will set up thy seed after
> thee, which shall proceed out of thy bowels, and
> I will establish his kingdom.

> He shall build an house for my name, and I will stablish the throne of his kingdom forever.

> I will be his father, and he shall be my son. If he commit iniquity, I will chasten him with the rod of men, and with the stripes of the children of men:

> But my mercy shall not depart away from him, as I took it away from Saul, whom I put away before thee,

> And thine house and thy kingdom shall be established for ever before thee: thy throne shall be established for ever.

Is there a contradiction between the various passages? Is the Davidic Covenant conditional in one Scripture and unconditional in another? The Eternal Security teachers do not quote the conditional passages I have quoted.

This passage they quote does not teach unconditional salvation, as they claim. God promised David that his kingdom would not end, as Saul's did. God promised: "I will set up thy seed after thee." Hebrew authorities say this is used in the *collective sense.*

> I will set up thy seed after thee, — used collectively for the whole descendants.... The chain of Messianic promises which for ages had been broken...was now renewed by the addition of a new and important link.... This is the oath which God sware by His holiness to David—the covenant which He made with him respecting the perpetuity of his royal seed and kingdom.[1]

God carried out His threats against Solomon and Israel for breaking His covenant, but He always found a faithful remnant through whom He kept His promise to David.

It is a dangerous and deceptive error to teach unconditional salvation from this Scripture. If

---

[1] *Jamieson, Fausset, Brown Commentary.*

Solomon did not obey the covenant's if-conditions, David said: "He will cast thee off forever." Let those consider this who believe they are eternally saved and yet continue to break God's covenant of salvation by their persistence in sin.

Salvation is of the Jews. The Davidic Covenant was of the Jews. The Davidic Covenant was conditional. Multitudes of Jews will never be saved because they continually broke the Jewish covenants of salvation.

7

The If-Condition in the Prophets

I DO NOT WISH to weary the reader with too many of these if-texts, so will not deal with them all. We shall look at a few more in the prophets to see how often God stressed this condition, and that it was an essential part of the covenant agreement. It was a qualification providing that when one does not perform a required act or acts, the promise is not operative. Compliance with the if-terms was required before the covenant would become effective. These if-terms specified not only obedience to the covenant laws but that they must be *continually* obeyed.

The Bible is based on a system of moral law easily understood by men. As in human covenants, so also in the divine—*breach of covenant* means forfeiture of covenant rights. Upon performance of the conditions, God, the Covenantor, assumed the obligations that became binding on His part. He was the Oath-Bound God. The nonperformance of the conditions would nullify and set aside the covenant for the covenant breakers. God is ready and willing to perform His part . . . if.

During the days of the prophet Azariah, there was a time of revival, prosperity, and peace in Israel because they obeyed this prophet who had warned King Asa:

> The Lord is with you, while ye be with him; and
> *if* ye seek him, he will be found of you; but *if*
> ye forsake him, he will forsake you. (II Chron.
> 15:1, 2)

> *If* my people, which are called by my name, shall
> humble themselves, and pray, and seek my face,
> and turn from their wicked ways; then will I
> hear from heaven...and will heal their land.
> (II Chron. 7:14)

King Hezekiah, after the Assyrian captivity,
warned Israel of the penalties attached to a broken
covenant. He told them about their fathers who had
suffered divine punishments because of breach of
covenant. He reminded them of sad events in Israel's
history because of their covenant transgressions. His
appeal to them was based on God's covenant-if:

> For *if* ye turn again unto the Lord...the Lord
> your God is gracious and merciful, and will not
> turn away his face from you, *if* ye return unto
> him.

The people accepted the covenant invitation and
"there was great joy in Jerusalem" (II Chron. 30:1–
26).

In Nehemiah's time there was a "remnant...left
of the captivity"; and when Nehemiah desired to rebuild the wall of Jerusalem, he reminded God of His
covenant-if: "Remember, I beseech thee, the word
that thou commandest thy servant Moses, saying,
...If ye turn unto me, and keep my commandments,
and do them; though there were of you cast out
unto the uttermost part of the heaven, yet will I
gather them from thence" (Neh. 1:8, 9). They obeyed
the condition, and God was with them to rebuild the
wall.

Isaiah stressed this if-factor in his message to
Israel:

> *If* ye be willing and obedient, ye shall eat the
> good of the land:

> But *if* ye refuse and rebel, ye shall be devoured
> with the sword: for the mouth of the Lord hath
> spoken it. (Isa. 1:19, 20)

Jeremiah, in his tearful pleadings to save Israel
from the deceptive security promised by the false
prophets, told them:

> For *if* ye thoroughly amend your ways and your
> doings; *if* ye thoroughly execute judgment be-
> tween a man and his neighbor;

> *If* ye oppress not the stranger, the fatherless, and
> the widow...neither walk after other gods to
> your hurt:

> Then will I cause you to dwell in this place, in
> the land that I gave to your fathers, for ever
> and ever. (Jer. 7:5–7)

Jeremiah, in his effort to save Israel from na-
tional disaster, repeated this if-warning twelve times
in chapters 12:16, 17; 15:19; 17:24–27; 18:8–10; 22:4,
5; 26:3, 4. But the people believed the false prophets
and did not obey Jeremiah's "ifs." And God's vengeance left their country in ruins, and the people
in slavery and death.

There was often a conflict between the true
prophets and the false prophets who did not require
obedience to God's commandments. They allowed the
people to continue in their sins. God said their
prophesied false security was a "horrible thing"...
"and my people love to have it so" (Jer. 5:30, 31).
They said that Jeremiah's prophesied judgments
would not come (Jer. 14:13–15). The people told the
prophets: "Speak unto us smooth things" (Isa. 30:
10). The false prophets told them the smooth things.
What could be smoother than to tell them they could
continue in their sins and that they and their nation
would be saved?

This delusion of security was widespread over
Israel. The Jews believed they were the predestinat-

ed heirs of Abraham and forever secure in the for-
tunes of the Abrahamic Covenant. "They cannot
imagine that the time will ever come when . . . the
State would come to an end." They thought they
were "secure, and can go about sinning with im-
punity" (Driver). The true prophets always tried to
save the people from the "lying words" and the spell
of false security cast over them by the false prophets. The false prophets gave the people a false
assurance.

> When the righteous turneth from his righteous-
> ness, and committeth iniquity, he shall even die
> thereby.
>
> But *if* the wicked turn from his wickedness, and
> do that which is lawful and right, *he shall live
> thereby.* (Ezek. 33:18, 19)

Ezekiel knew nothing about a predestination that
keeps the sinner while he persists in sin. He said
the sinner must turn from his sin and do that which
is lawful and right, or he would die. The covenant
conditions carried all the way through to the end
of the Old Testament. Zechariah told the priest
Joshua:

> Thus saith the Lord of hosts; *If* thou wilt walk in
> my ways, and *if* thou wilt keep my charge, then
> thou shalt also judge my house, and shalt also
> keep my courts. (Zech. 3:7)

The last covenant-if in the Old Testament is in
Malachi 2:2.

> And now, O ye priests, this commandment is for
> you. *If* ye will not hear, and *if* ye will not lay it
> to heart, to give glory unto my name, saith the
> Lord of hosts, I will even send a curse upon you.

The commentaries of Professors Delitzsch and
Driver, quoted before for the meaning of the if-
condition, also agree that this "if" has the same con-

ditional sense in the prophets. The *Pulpit Commentary, Jamieson, Fausset, Brown Commentary,* and other leading critical commentaries agree.

So, from God's "if" to Cain, to Malachi's "if" to the priests, we have seen a long chain of 63 if-texts to prove that the Jewish covenants were conditional. And New Testament salvation is founded on these covenants. Isn't it strange that Eternal Security teachers give no importance to a condition that God has emphasized more than 63 times in these Old Testament covenants upon which salvation was established?

We go now to the New Testament and shall see there the same emphasis on this if-condition for salvation that we found in the Old Testament. Salvation was not conditional in the Old Testament and unconditional in the New. By a *rule of unity,* both Testaments are one.

Many leading Biblical authorities give full support to the following statement:

> There is much reason for believing that the habit ...of treating the hermeneutics of the New Testament separately from the Old, has occasioned the misunderstanding of some important doctrines of Holy Writ. The language and style in which certain New Testament teachings are expressed are so manifestly modeled after Old Testament forms of statement, that they cannot be properly explained without a minute and thorough apprehension of the import of the older Scripture.[1]

Salvation came from Jewish covenants. Each of these covenants was an If-Covenant. We shall now see that the New Covenant is an If-Covenant.

---

[1] *Biblical Hermeneutics,* Terry, M. S., p. 466. 1895.

8

The If-Condition in the

Teachings of Jesus

JESUS CONTINUED THE EMPHASIS of the Old Testament if-condition about salvation. We shall see the same frequency of the if-emphasis in the New Covenant that we saw in the Old. The Bible uses considerable repetition of truths about our salvation "though ye know them, and be established in the present truth" (II Pet. 1: 10–15).

God's covenant plan was projected on an if-basis. God specified His "if" for Cain, and this if-importance was followed with successive repetition by Moses, Joshua, David, Solomon, Hezekiah, Nehemiah, Isaiah, Jeremiah, Ezekiel, Zechariah, and Malachi. As we reason from one covenant to another, the evidence increases for the belief that the conditional moral structure of one covenant is essentially the same as that of another covenant. The covenants embodied promises and conditions; and when these covenants passed to future generations, they were not stripped of their "ifs."

The Abrahamic Covenant was an If-Covenant. The Sinaitic Covenant was an If-Covenant. The Davidic Covenant was an If-Covenant. I will now try to prove to you that the New Covenant is an If-Covenant.

Jesus was a Jew. He lived as a Jew. He was born in fulfillment of Jewish covenants, although He was promised from the foundation of the world. He was the "son of David, the son of Abraham" (Matt. 1:1; Acts 13:23; Rom. 1:3; Gal. 3:16; II Tim. 2:8). As the Seed of the covenant fathers, Jesus fulfilled the covenants of salvation made to Abraham and David. In the process of covenant development, the covenants moved toward Christ for their fulfillment. The New Covenant is founded on the Abrahamic-Davidic Covenants. Each covenant that followed the Abrahamic Covenant was an outgrowth and further expansion of the Abrahamic.

At the beginning of Christ's ministry, He taught the conditional nature of salvation when He delivered His marvelous system of moral law in the Sermon on the Mount.

> For *if* ye forgive men their trespasses, your heavenly Father will also forgive you:
>
> But *if* ye forgive not men their trespasses, neither will your Father forgive your trespasses. (Matt. 6:14, 15)

In the Greek New Testament, "if" has the same conditional meaning in these texts as in the English. It is used to express a condition. It is also understood in this sense by law courts. Professor M. M. Bryant of Columbia University made a study to see how words are interpreted in law courts and the part they play in legal decisions. Professor Bryant put the result of this study, with legal citations, in a book, *English in the Law Courts* (F. Unger Co. 1962). On page 230, in law courts, when "if" is used to express a condition, it has the same meaning as in general usage: "in case that," "allowing or supposing that." As Bible covenants are legal transactions, their ifs would be interpreted in law courts as would be "if" in any other document.

In chapter one, I quoted from the popular Calvinist writer, Arthur W. Pink: "Personally we have no more to do with our spiritual birth than we had with our natural birth." Now here's a quote from the same author on these if-texts in Matthew 6:14, 15:

> "If ye forgive men their trespasses, your heavenly Father will also forgive you." Very searching indeed are these words, constituting a severe test of discipleship, a test which excludes from the ranks of God's children those...refusing to forgive those who injure them.
>
> First, our forgiveness is a *condition* or necessary qualification if we are to receive the continued pardon of God.... "But if ye forgive not men their trespasses, neither will your Father forgive your trespasses." Unspeakably solemn is this, and each of us needs diligently to search his heart in the light of it....
>
> It will be seen then, that the passage we have been considering presents a very real test of discipleship.[1] (his italics)

The two statements are inconsistent and contradictory. A lawyer, using such contradictory language, would lose his case in court.

I will not argue from all the if-statements Jesus made. A few are sufficient.

> Then said Jesus unto his disciples, *If* any man will come after me, let him deny himself, and take up his cross, and follow me.
>
> For whosoever will save his life shall lose it: and whosoever will lose his life for my sake shall find it.
>
> For what is a man profited, if he shall gain the whole world, and lose his own soul? or what shall

---

[1] *An Exposition of the Sermon on the Mount*, Pink, Arthur W., pp. 168–171. Baker, 1959.

a man give in exchange for his soul? (Matt. 16: 24–26)

The if-statement of Jesus on this occasion is in a context about a man losing his soul. So, we have evidence here that Jesus taught salvation to be conditional upon a man denying himself, and taking up his cross, and following Him continuously.

Jesus taught here that "whosoever" obeyed the conditions for salvation would "save his life," and whosoever did not obey the conditions would "lose his own soul." The grammar of the Greek New Testament in this if-text means: "Begin now to follow me, and continue doing so." [2]

True faith reveals itself in continual obedience to Christ's conditions for salvation. Unbelief manifests itself in continually disobeying these conditions. Christ does not give eternal life for a momentary surge of emotion or the fleeting impulse of a single act of faith. Jesus told about some people who "endure but for a time" (Mark 4: 17); "but he that endureth to the end shall be saved" (Matt. 10: 22).

It is evident that Christ was severe in His requirements for discipleship. He reminds us of what God required of Abraham: "Get thee out of thy country, and from thy kindred, and from thy father's house. . . ." Similar conditions are given in Luke 14: 25–35:

And there went great multitudes with him: and he turned and said unto them,

If any man come to me, and hate not his father, and mother, and wife, and children, and brethren, and sisters, yea, and his own life also, he cannot be my disciple. . . .

So likewise, whosoever he be of you that forsaketh not all that he hath, he cannot be my disciple.

-----

[2] *A Manual Grammar of the Greek New Testament*, Dana & Mantey, p. 300. 25th edition; Macmillan, 1960.

Salt is good: but if the salt have lost his savour, wherewith shall it be seasoned?

It is neither fit for the land, nor yet for the dung-hill; but men cast it out. He that hath ears to hear, let him hear.

Jesus, with striking emphasis, repeated that he who does not obey the forsake-all condition "cannot be my disciple." Jesus then used the illustration of salt losing its savor and He used it in a context about conditions for salvation. "In this place the salt appears to denote disciples and the idea to be: genuine disciples are an excellent thing, valuable as salt to a corrupt world, but spurious disciples are as utterly worthless as salt which has lost its savor" (*Expositors Greek Testament*). "Without *absolute surrender of self,* the contest is hopeless" (*Jamieson, Fausset, and Brown Commentary*). The *Pulpit Commentary,* commenting on Christ's salt statement here, says:

Here "salt" stands for the spirit of self-sacrifice, self-renunciation. When in a man, or in a nation, or in a Church, that salt is savorless, then that spirit is dead; there is no hope remaining for the man, for the people, or the Church. The lesson was a general one—it was meant to sink into each listener's heart; but the Master's sad gaze was fixed...on the temple of Jerusalem where his glory-presence used to dwell. *Men cast it out.* Jesus could hear the armed tramp of the Roman legions of the year 70 as they cast out his people from their holy land.

Further authoritative support for this view is found in *The Life and Times of Jesus the Messiah.*[3] As savorless salt is not fit for the dunghill, so also many who profess salvation are unfit for the Kingdom of God.

Let the reader consider Christ's plain statements about conditional salvation, and then read what the

---

[3] Alfred Edersheim, V. 2, pp. 305–306. Eerdmans, 1953.

Eternal Security teachers say: "There is no need for
continuous faith on the part of the saved person" —
"The predestinated are saved without regard to what
they may or may not do." The teachings of Christ
repudiated this deceptive assurance. Christ revealed
that multitudes are hopelessly deceived, but that
they will finally see at the judgment they were de-
luded with a false security about their salvation
(Matt. 8:11, 12).

We look now at a few more of Jesus' if-statements
in John:

> Then said Jesus to those Jews which believed on
> him, *If* ye continue in my word, then are ye my
> disciples indeed....
>
> They answered and said unto him, Abraham is
> our father. Jesus saith unto them, If ye were Abra-
> ham's children, ye would do the works of Abra-
> ham....
>
> If God were your father, ye would love me....
>
> He that is of God heareth God's words: ye there-
> fore hear them not, because ye are not of God....
>
> Verily, verily, I say unto you, *If* a man keep my
> saying, he shall never see death. (John 8:31–51)

We now look at Calvin's entire exposition of
Christ's conditional statement in John 8:31.

> "If ye continue in my word." Here Christ warns
> them, in the first place, that it is not enough for
> any one to have begun well, if their progress to
> the end does not correspond to it; and for this
> reason he exhorts to perseverance in the faith
> those who have tasted of his doctrine. When he
> says that they who are firmly rooted *in his word,*
> so as to *continue* in him, *will truly be his disci-*
> *ples,* he means that many profess to be his *dis-*
> *ciples* who yet are not so in reality, and have no
> right to be accounted such. He distinguishes his
> followers from hypocrites by this mark, that they
> who falsely boasted of faith give way as soon

as they have entered into the course, or at least in the middle of it; but believers persevere constantly to the end. If, therefore, we wish that Christ should reckon us to be his disciples, we must endeavor to persevere.[4] (The emphasis is Calvin's.)

Calvin sounds like an Arminian here, doesn't he? In checking Calvin's commentaries on various if-texts, he seemed vague and inconsistent to me, but this was one of the few clear statements I found. But you must be careful reading Calvin because he gives it to you in one place, and takes it away in another. Like Augustine, he is inconsistent and self-contradictory. Notice in the above statement that Calvin used "if" twice.

The Jews boasted to Christ about their security in the Abrahamic Covenant: "Abraham is our father." But Jesus unmasked them as being hypocrites with: "*If* ye were Abraham's children, ye would *do* the *works* of Abraham." It was by the Abrahamic works-test that Jesus proved them to be of "your father the devil"; and, "The lusts of your father ye will do"; and, "Ye do the deeds of your father" (John 8: 39–44).

We have seen there were four conditions to the Abrahamic Covenant and that Abraham obeyed and continually kept these conditions. This was what Jesus referred to as the "works of Abraham." With this, Jesus showed the same moral conditions of the Abrahamic Covenant to be in effect for the New Covenant. It was not conditional for Abraham and unconditional for Abraham's children.

To these Jews who smugly believed they were predestinated to the eternal Abrahamic kingdom, Christ applied two other tests: the sin-test and the

---

[4] *Commentary on the Gospel According to John*, V. I, pp. 340–341. Eerdmans, 1949.

Word-test. "Verily, verily, I say unto you, *Whosoever* committeth sin is the servant [slave] of sin." "He that is of God heareth God's words: ye therefore hear them not, because ye are not of God" (John 8:34, 47). Jesus said that anyone who persisted in sin was of the devil, and did the lusts and deeds of the devil. The devil "abode not in the truth" (John 8:44).

"By their fruits ye shall know them." This is a test that Christ applied to false prophets and false believers, as the context of Matthew 7:15–27 shows. Jesus used three tests on these Jews: the works-test, the sin-test, the Word-test. And even John Calvin, in the above quotation, said that Christ "distinguishes his followers from hypocrites by this mark."

The Jews claimed eternal security in the Abrahamic Covenant because they were the sons of Abraham, and, "once a son, always a son." Jesus told us a remarkable story about this father-son relationship in Luke 16:22–26:

> And it came to pass, that the beggar died, and was carried by the angels into Abraham's bosom: the rich man also died, and was buried:
>
> And in hell he lift up his eyes, being in torments, and seeth Abraham afar off, and Lazarus in his bosom.
>
> And he cried and said, *Father* Abraham, have mercy on me. . . .
>
> But Abraham said, *Son*, remember that thou in thy lifetime receivedst thy good things, and likewise Lazarus evil things: but now he is comforted, and thou art tormented.
>
> And beside all this, between us and you there is a great gulf fixed: so that they which would pass from hence to you cannot; neither can they pass to us, that would come from thence.

This Jew, claiming birth and sonship in the Abrahamic Covenant, appealed to Abraham as "Father." This was acknowledged by Abraham who called him "Son." But the father was in Paradise forever and the son was in hell forever. No one could ever pass the great gulf that separated them.

Christ's teaching enraged the Jews more than did His miracles. They had Him crucified because of His teaching—the teaching that He was the Son of God and Saviour of the world; teaching that exposed them—Abraham's covenant sons—as children of the devil; teaching that made salvation conditional with a big "if"; teaching that put a covenant son of Abraham in torment forever; teaching that had them—"the *children of the kingdom* . . . cast into outer darkness: [where] there shall be weeping and gnashing of teeth" (Matt. 8:12).

Some teach that these Jews who are cast out of the Kingdom will get another chance to enter it. But there is no evidence that the Jews understood it that way. Nor will it be so understood by the Jews when they are cast out. Why do they weep and gnash their teeth if they get another chance? Some interpreters make "outer darkness" to be different from "damnation," but the Jews didn't understand it that way.[5]

On this if-condition in John 8:31, Professor A. T. Robertson, the foremost Greek authority of modern times, wrote:

Your future loyalty to my teaching will prove the reality of your present profession. So the conclusion of this future condition is put in the present tense. As then, so now.... Continuance in the word (teaching) proves the sincerity or in-

[5] See II Peter 2:17; Jude 13. *Expository Dictionary of New Testament Words*, Vine, W. E., V. 1, p. 268. Oliphants, 1948.

sincerity of the profession. It is the acid test of life.[6]

Jesus made everything conditional upon obedient love. Everything comes from God's free grace, but obedience and faith make it possible for God to give this grace to those who qualify for it. Jesus made this clear with more ifs. "*If* ye love me, keep my commandments." "*If* a man love me, he will keep my words: and my Father will love him" (John 14: 15, 23).

> *If* a man abide not in me, he is cast forth as a branch, and is withered; and men gather them, and cast them into the fire, and they are burned.

> *If* ye keep my commandments, ye shall abide in my love; even as I have kept my Father's commandments, and abide in his love. (John 15:6, 10)

> *If* any man willeth to do his will, he shall know the teaching.   (John 7:17, RV)

On the latter reference, Dr. Robertson wrote: The conditional is used here with "full force of *thelo,* to will, to wish." Christ's if-essential demands the continual wish, will, obedience, and love of those who claim salvation. God's covenant of salvation is an eternal-life guarantee to all who "abide" in it. It has Christ's "verily, verily," behind it. Christ is the *surety* of it (Heb. 7:22). It is validated by God's "oath." And God has put His "yea-amen" to it (II Cor. 1:20). It is a "*sure* word of prophecy" to all who continually believe (II Pet. 1:19).

The "ifs" in Christ's teaching is sufficient evidence for our conclusion that salvation is conditional. The authority of the Greek New Testament fully corroborates our view. True love and faith working together have continuous action in Christ.

---

[6] *Word Pictures in the New Testament*, V. 5, p. 149. Broadman Press, 1932.

Every time Jesus asked a person to follow him he used the...present imperative. "And he says to him, Follow me." Mt. 9:9. That is, begin now to follow me, and continue doing so. When the present imperative is used, it denotes *continuous* or *repeated* action.[7]

The Greek New Testament teaches in John 3:15; 5:24; 6:35; 6:54; 11:25: "Whosoever is continually believing has eternal life" — "He that believes on me continually shall never thirst" — "He who keeps eating my flesh and drinking my blood has eternal life" — "He that persistently believes in me, though he were dead, yet shall he live." The idea is of an action begun, and to be continued. Jesus taught in the parable of the sower that the good seed *continues* to grow until it brings forth good fruit. Other seed does not continue to grow because it is choked by the cares and pleasures of life and does not bring forth fruit (Luke 8:14, 15).

I am the true vine.... *If* a man abide not in me, he is cast forth as a branch, and is withered; and men gather them, and cast them into the fire, and they are burned. (John 15:1, 6)

Christ here again makes salvation conditional upon abiding continually in Him. "There is nothing for a broken off branch to do but wither and die." ..."The apostles are thus vividly warned against presumption" (Robertson). *"He is cast forth.* The aorist tense. Lit., *was* cast forth. The aorist, denoting a momentary act, indicates that it was cast forth at the moment it ceased to abide in the vine. *Forth*-signifies *from the vineyard; outside"* (Vincent).

The continue-in-sin doctrine is refuted by Christ's continue-in-faith doctrine. He who continues to sin falls into an eternal death-trap. There is no uncon-

---

[7] *A Manual Grammar of the Greek New Testament*, Dana & Mantey, p. 300. 25th edition; Macmillan, 1960.

ditional salvation when God uses His pruning-knife. Jesus clearly taught us here that the teaching of "once in the Vine, always in the Vine" is a great deception. (We shall see more of this in Romans 11.)

Two men asked Jesus what they must do to inherit eternal life. One asked: "What good thing shall I *do*, that I may have eternal life?" Jesus replied: "*If* thou wilt enter into life, *keep* the commandments" (Matt. 19:17). The other inquirer asked: "Master, what shall I *do* to inherit eternal life?" Jesus directed him to the commandment: "Thou shalt love the Lord thy God with all thine heart, and with all thy soul, and with all thy strength, and with all thy mind; and thy neighbour as thyself." Then Jesus added: "This *do*, and thou shalt live [eternally]."

Salvation is of the Jews. But no Jew could enter the Kingdom of God unless he continually obeyed the covenant commandments. That is what the King of the Jews said. The New Covenant salvation is an If-Covenant. The evidence demands this conclusion.

9

The If-Condition in the

Epistles of Paul

ROMANS

WE COME NOW to the 9th chapter of Romans and enter the stronghold of Augustine, Calvin, and the Eternal Security teachers. This is the passage most argued by them in defense of their predestination doctrine. So, let us give them a fair hearing. Let us not evade or twist anything as they often do. We shall examine the passage by fair rules of interpretation, and let truth be whatever it is. If salvation is unconditional, let us believe it.

These Roman texts do not disprove the long chain of if-facts we have seen all the way from Genesis. A *few* Scriptures do not disprove *many* Scriptures. The Bible is not a house divided against itself. The whole Bible is a unit of truth, and a true interpreter will impartially seek the truth in all parts of this unit. Each part fits into the whole unit. It is a vicious system of interpretation that picks and chooses those parts of Scripture that *seem* to affirm a doctrine but ignores other parts. Every false doctrine in Christianity today is defended by this method of interpretation.

Romans 9 does not teach differently about election or predestination than do other Scriptures about this doctrine. We must understand Paul in Romans 9 by Paul in his other Epistles. Paul is not at variance with himself, nor is he at variance with the if-condition of Moses, Jesus, and the prophets. When all the Scriptures on a doctrine are fairly examined, a single thought emerges and predominates.

This rule of unity has been grossly violated by Augustine, Calvin, and the Eternal Security teachers. And if they are allowed to do this, then as Young says in the Preface of his *Literal Translation of the Bible*: "We cannot deny the same privilege to others who may twist other passages in like manner." The hopeless mass of doctrinal confusion among Christian denominations today is the result of distorted interpretation.

Dr. F. W. Farrar, Dean of Canterbury, stands in the first rank of Bible scholars. He spent 20 years on his valuable work, *History of Interpretation.*[1]

He said on page 39:

> The misinterpretation of Scripture must be reckoned among the gravest calamities of Christendom.

The misinterpretation of election and predestination is among these grave calamities. Let us now get the facts and see why this is true.

First, it is highly important that we establish the definitions of election, predestination, and foreknowledge. In the Appendix you can see that the first rule of interpretation is the *Rule of Definition*. If you haven't studied the history of Christian doctrines, you may not know that the great doctrinal debates of the theologians since the second century were mostly disputes about the meaning of Biblical words.

---

[1] Baker, 1961.

Everything hangs on the meaning of words, and often they are dangerous things. Recently I heard a news commentator say: "The United Nations has been trying to define the word *aggression* for 15 years."

Many people, even some who call themselves Calvinists, do not know what election is. This is also true of some ministers.

The following definitions are from the highest authorities. Experts call these authorities "standard sources" of evidence.

> Election, (*eklektos*). Chosen, select—especially, of those whom God has chosen from the generality of mankind and drawn to himself.[2]

> Election, (*eklektos*). literally, signifies picked out, chosen (*ek*, from, *lego*, to gather, pick out). While Christ's Death was sufficient for all men, and is effective in the case of the elect, yet men are treated as responsible, being capable of the will and power to choose.[3]

> Election, (*eklektos*). univ. choice, select, i.e., the best of its kind or class.[4]

In the world of Greek scholarship, Moulton's & Milligan's *The Vocabulary of the Greek New Testament* is recognized as the "final court of appeals" on New Testament usage because it shows from the papyri and inscriptions how Bible words were used in the first-century Greek world. On page 196 of this highest New Testament authority, the term election (*eklektos*) is defined as

> "selected, i, e, of a better quality than the rest."

---

[2] *A Greek-English Lexicon of the New Testament*, Arndt & Gingrich, p. 242. University of Chicago Press, 1957.

[3] *Expository Dictionary of New Testament Words*, Vine, W. E., V. 2, pp. 21–22. Oliphants Ltd., London, 1948.

[4] *A Greek-English Lexicon of the New Testament*, Thayer, J. H., p. 197. 1889.

o

The *International Standard Bible Encyclopedia* is widely referred to as "the best Bible encyclopedia." I quote: [5]

> ...election never appears as a violation of human will. For never in the Bible is man treated as irresponsible. In the Bible the relation of the human and Divine wills is inscrutable; the reality of both is assured. Never is the doctrine presented apart from a moral context.

More authorities could be quoted but these should be sufficient. We look now at the meaning of "predestination."

> Predestination (*proorizo*). *to predetermine, decide beforehand.* [6]

> Predestinate (*pro-orizo*). This verb is to be distinguished from *pro-ginosko,* to foreknow; the latter has special reference to the persons foreknown by God; *pro-orizo* (predestination) has special reference to that to which the subjects of His foreknowledge are predestinated. [7]

During my researches on Biblical subjects I found *Hastings Dictionary of the Bible* in the reference sections of great libraries. It has been an outstanding authority for two generations. I quote on predestination: [8]

> The English word 'predestination' in the AV is, in the few cases in which it occurs (Rom. 8: 29–30; Eph. 1: 5, 11) exchanged in the RV for 'foreordain,' a return to the use of the older Versions. The Greek word *pro-orizo* (predestination) con-

---

[5] V. 2, p. 927. Eerdmans, 1952.

[6] *A Greek-English Lexicon of the New Testament,* Arndt & Gingrich, p. 716. University of Chicago Press, 1957.

Thayer's Greek-English Lexicon of the New Testament, p. 541.

[7] *Expository Dictionary of New Testament Words,* Vine, W. E., V. 3, p. 203.

[8] pp. 747–49. 1918 edition.

veys the simple idea of defining or determining beforehand. . . .

'election' and 'foreknowledge' to salvation seem to have much the same meaning. Yet in usage a certain distinction is made. It may perhaps be stated thus, that 'election' denotes the Divine choice simply, while 'foreordain' has generally (in sense of 'predestinate') a reference to the end which the foreordination has in view. Those 'foreknown' are afterwards described as God's 'elect' (Rom. 8: 30–33). This striking passage further shows how, *in foreordaining the end, God likewise foreordains all the steps that lead to it* ('foreknew' — 'foreordained' — 'called' — 'justified' 'glorified') . . . .

As little does the Apostle attempt to show the compatibility of the Divine foreordination with *human freedom,* but habitually assumes that the one is not, and cannot be, in violation of the other. . . .

Scripture itself, with all its emphasis on foreordination, never speaks of a foreordination to death, or of a reprobation of human beings apart from their own sins. (my emphasis)

You may be interested to read a few comments on predestination from *The International Standard Bible Encyclopaedia.*[9]

The predestined certainty of God's gracious work in Christ was not meant to perplex men, but to encourage and reassure all who trust in His grace. . . .

The needful thing is to understand, so far as may be, the nature of the cooperation that takes place between the Divine and the human factors or elements, which latter factors include natural capacity, disposition and development, working under grace. It must be carefully observed that nothing in Scripture points to any personal and inexorable

---

[9] V. 4, pp. 2435–2436. Eerdmans, 1952. (Used by permission.)

predestination to reprobation.... A non-election there may be, of course, but not in any sense that annuls full personal responsibility for coming short of life everlasting. The appeal of Scripture from first to last is to men as free.

Calvin's strange way of putting the matter was, "Man therefore falls, God's Providence so ordaining, but he falls by his own fault."

Calvin's mode of defining predestination was as the eternal decree of God, by which He had decided with Himself what is to become of each and every individual. For all, he maintains, are not created in like condition; but eternal life is foreordained for some, eternal condemnation for others.

Calvin confesses that this is a "horrible decree," and it is not surprising to find competent theologians in our time denying such a form of predestinarianism any place in the teachings of St. Paul.

It is but fair to Calvin to remember — for superficial acquaintance with his teachings is far from rare — that he, in the strongest manner, maintained Divine sovereignty to be that of Divine wisdom, righteousness, and love, and expressly rejected the notion of absolute power.... Calvin expressly taught that no *cause* or ground but God's unconditional will was to be sought; but he feebly tried to save Divine will from sheer omnipotence by saying that God is˙a law to Himself; and the notion of sovereignty continued to be presented in ways quite absolute and irresponsible. (my emphasis)

Now, what does "foreknowledge" mean? We go again to the Greek lexicons.

Foreknowledge (*pro-ginosko, pro-gnosis*), to know before (*pro*, before, *ginosko*, to know),... the foreknowledge of God is the basis of His foreordaining counsels.... God's foreknowledge involves His electing grace, but this does not preclude human will. He foreknows the exercise of faith which brings salvation.[10]

Foreknowledge (*pro-ginosko*), to have knowledge of beforehand; to foreknow...whom he (God) foreknew, namely, that they would love him, or (with reference to what follows) whom he foreknew to be fit to be conformed to the image of his Son...Rom. 8: 29.[11]

Foreknowledge (*pro-ginosko*), to know beforehand, foreknow.[12]

The rule of definition is the first and most important of interpretive laws. In these definitions of election, predestination, and foreknowledge there is no evidence for unconditional salvation. None whatever. Not even a hint. So, now that we have our definitions fixed, and have cleared the way, we approach these texts in Romans 9 that have been a doctrinal tempest for theologians during the past 16 centuries of bitter debate. Here's their first argument for unconditional salvation:

9. For this is the word of promise, At this time will I come, and Sarah shall have a son.

10. And not only this; but when Rebecca also had conceived by one, even our father Isaac;

11. (For the children being not yet born, neither having done good or evil, that the purpose of God according to election might stand, not of works, but of him that calleth;)

12. It was said unto her, The elder shall serve the younger.

13. As it is written, Jacob have I loved, but Esau have I hated.

---

[10] *Expository Dictionary of New Testament Words*, Vine, W. E., V. 2, p. 119.

[11] *Thayer's English-Greek Lexicon of the New Testament*, p. 538.

[12] *Manual Greek Lexicon of the New Testament*, Abbott-Smith, p. 379. Scribner's, 1936.

Our opponents, using these verses to support their doctrine of unconditional salvation, say it was God's elective purpose to love Jacob and hate Esau. They point out that God predestinated them to be loved and hated when they were "not yet born, neither having done good or evil." The reason for this elective choice, they say, lies in the mysterious sovereign will of God, and is therefore beyond the power of human thought to penetrate. As Augustine said, "The more difficult this is to understand, the more laudable is the faith that believes it."

Calvin said there is a deep mystery to this "horrible decree" that caused God to love Jacob and hate Esau, without regard to anything they could do or could not do for their salvation. And Calvin held that God's love and wisdom was the cause of His predestinating choice in loving and hating them, without regard to anything they could do or could not do. God's love and wisdom, then, issued this "horrible decree." Could *human* love and wisdom do such a horrible thing? Here in Romans 13:10, Paul said: "Love worketh no ill." Then, can divine love work such horrible ill to men?

Why then did God love Jacob and hate Esau? First, it will help if we can clear up the meaning of "hated." Greek authorities say:

> Hated. The expression is intentionally strong as an expression of moral antipathy. Compare Matt. 6:24; Lu. 14:26. No idea of malice is implied of course.[13]

Professor A. T. Robertson wrote in his *Word Pictures in the New Testament:* [14]

> This language sounds a bit harsh to us. ... It is possible that the word *miseo* (hate) did not al-

---

[13] *Vincent's Word Studies*, V. 3, p. 104. Eerdmans, 1957.
[14] V. 4, p. 382.

ways carry the full force of what we mean by "hate."

W. E. Vine, in his *Expository Dictionary of New Testament Words*[15] has the following definition which is supported by the Abbott-Smith *Manual Greek Lexicon of the New Testament*.[16] Vine said this "hated" is used:

> ...of relative preference for one thing over another, by way of expressing either aversion from, or disregard for, the claims of one person or thing relatively to those of another, Mt. 6:24; Lu. 16:13.

Why then did God have this "relative preference" for Jacob, and this "relative disregard" for Esau? Remember the definitions from the leading lexicons about *election* which signify "choice, select, i.e., the best of its kind or class"—"selected, i.e., of a better quality than the rest."

God's reasons for His choice of Jacob over Esau are reasons found in the characters of these two men, and not reasons in a mysterious sovereign will. Let us take a glance at the characters of the two men and see if this could be true.

God appeared to Jacob and revealed himself to him; and Jacob vowed a vow to serve God (Gen. 28:10–22). Jacob honored his father and mother and obeyed their wishes not to marry a heathen woman. His conscience protested against participating in the tricks his mother taught him (Gen. 27:11–13). Jacob was a man of faith (Heb. 11:21). He was mighty in prayer and prevailed with God, and was changed from Jacob ("supplanter") to "Israel," which is the great covenant name of the Jews. Jacob was a man who saw God "face to face" (Gen. 32:24–30). There were

---

[15] V. 2, p. 198.
[16] p. 293.

defects in his character but he was changed into a great saint and covenant partner with God. Throughout the Scriptures, Jehovah is "the God of Abraham, Isaac, and Jacob."

In contrast to Jacob, consider Esau: He "despised" his birthright and sold it for "one morsel of meat" (Heb. 12:16). This indicated his low estimate of spiritual values and his desire for the pleasure of appetite. He married heathen wives which was a "grief" to his parents (Gen. 26:34, 35). He was a man of unbelief and debased character. His whole evil character was gathered and flashed at us in two words: "fornicator" and "profane." The word profane (*bebelos*) means "unclean" and "godless." It also means "that which lacks all relationship or affinity to God" (Vine).

> Lest there be any fornicator, or profane person, as Esau, who for one morsel of meat sold his birthright.

> For ye know how that afterward, when he would have inherited the blessing, he was rejected: for he found no place of repentance, though he sought it carefully with tears. (Heb. 12:16, 17)

Our opponents argue that God made His choice between Jacob and Esau before they were born— before they had done good or evil. But this need not cause anyone to stumble. God foreknows all things as perfectly as He can ever know them. He would not be God if He did not have this foreknowledge. Even the heathen claim their gods possess this omniscience.

After telling us about Jacob and Esau, Paul continued his thought in verses 14–18.

> 14. What shall we say then? Is there unrighteousness with God? God forbid.

15. For he saith to Moses, I will have mercy on whom I will have mercy, and I will have compassion on whom I will have compassion.

16. So then it is not of him that willeth, nor of him that runneth, but of God that sheweth mercy.

17. For the Scripture saith unto Pharaoh, Even for this same purpose have I raised thee up, that I might shew my power in thee, and that my name might be declared throughout the earth.

18. Therefore hath he mercy on whom he will have mercy, and whom he will he hardeneth.

"Is there unrighteousness with God? God forbid." God is not unrighteous for choosing Jacob, who as a "prince" had "power with God" and "prevailed"—a man who was transformed into the mighty "Israel" when God revealed himself to him face to face. Nor was God unrighteous for rejecting the fornicator and profane Esau who joined himself to heathen.

The next point that Eternal Security teachers stress is verse 15: "I will have mercy on whom I will have mercy, and I will have compassion on whom I will have compassion." This statement is in a context about Jacob, Esau, and Pharaoh. We have seen what an evil character Esau was, and Pharaoh was worse.

Dr. Robertson, in his *Word Pictures in the New Testament*,[17] pointed out that "Pharaoh hardened his own heart also (Ex. 8: 15, 32; 9: 34)." God gives men up to "their own" hardness of heart (Rom. 1: 24–28). Pharaoh wasn't born hardened, nor was Hitler, Khrushchev, or any sinner. They reached the hardened state through progressive stages of unbelief and

---

[17] V. 4, p. 383. Broadman Press.

disobedience. We preachers have seen many sinners sink deeper and deeper into this hardened state as they willfully and persistently rejected God and His truth. The Apostle James (1: 14–16) specified three stages to this deadly progression:

> But every man is tempted, when he is drawn away of *his own lust,* and enticed.

> Then when lust hath conceived, it bringeth forth sin: and sin, when it is finished, bringeth forth death.

> Do not err, my beloved brethren.

Everything moves ever onward to its climax. Every cancer has a small beginning. Every hardened heart began with "his own lust" and develops by the same satanic means until it is full grown. Don't think it began in the predestinating counsel of God. There are many speculative ideas about the origin of sin but James set us straight, and said it begins when the sinner follows Satan's lure "of his own lust." Sinners love sin, as Esau and Pharaoh did.

This hardening of heart is given repeated emphasis in Scripture. Nehemiah said the Israelites "hardened their necks . . . and refused to obey" (9: 16, 17). The Israelites continually disobeyed the warnings of the prophets and "hardened their necks, like the neck of their fathers . . . and rejected his statutes, and his covenant" (II Kings 17: 14, 15). Solomon said a sinner "hardeneth his neck" after being "often reproved" (Prov. 29: 1). Acts 19: 8, 9 says that many Jews were "hardened" after hearing Paul for "three months." Hebrews 3: 13 says sinners are "hardened through the deceitfulness of sin"; and verses 8, 15: "Today if ye hear his voice, harden not your hearts, as in the provocation . . . in the wilderness." Unbelievers harden their hearts after they hear the voice of God. This was true of Pharaoh.

God did not have mercy on Esau. He did not give
compassion to Pharaoh. But men are not predestinated robots. God has wise and good reasons for
giving mercy to some and withholding it from others.
Jesus and Paul used proof texts for their theology,
so let us consider three of many proofs which show
that God has reasons for granting His mercy.

1. God said He shows "mercy unto thousands of
them that love me, and keep my commandments"
(Ex. 20:6). Loving God and keeping His commandments are conditions for receiving His mercy.

2. The mother of Jesus said that God's "mercy
is on them that fear him from generation to generation" (Luke 1:50). Clearly, Mary understood that
fear of God was a condition of His mercy.

3. "He that despised Moses' law died without
mercy" (Heb. 10:28). Disrespect for Moses' law was
a cause for not receiving mercy. Those who respected it received mercy. Respectful obedience was
a condition. Those who obeyed Moses *could* have disobeyed, and those who disobeyed *could* have obeyed.
God does not give His mercy to "them that hate me"
(Deut. 5:9).

Esau could have obeyed God and received mercy.
But he despised his birthright. He despised his parents. He despised God. He did not receive God's mercy because he was a fornicator and profane person.
His evil life was not the result of his acting under
the impulses of a mysterious predestination. His profane acts were not the workings of foreordained
damnation. It was *Esau* who was profane. It was
Pharaoh who opposed God. God has mercy on whom
He will, but this mercy is not an *automatic* thing.
It is governed by righteous laws.

The Eternal Security teachers press hard on verse
16 in relation to Jacob, Esau, and Pharaoh. This
has been one of the most disputed texts in 16 cen-

turies of doctrinal debate. "So then it is not of him that willeth, nor of him that runneth, but of God that sheweth mercy."

We consider first: "not of him that willeth." Opposing teachers say this means that the wills of Jacob, Esau, and Pharaoh had no part in their eternal destinies. All is determined by sovereign will. As supporting evidence they quote John 1:13: "Which were born, not of blood, nor of the will of the flesh, nor of the will of man, but of God." But the preceding verses, which they neglect, upset this interpretation.

> He came unto his own, and his own received him not. But as many as received him, to them gave he power to become the sons of God, even to them that believe on his name.

To receive Him and to believe on His name were conditions for becoming sons of God. Can anyone do this without *willing* it? One must wreck the laws of language and logic to deny it.

Jesus came to "his own" and told them: "How often *would I* have gathered thy children together, as a hen doth gather her brood under her wings, and *ye would not*" (Luke 13:34). Observe the opposite thought: "would I"—"ye would not." By all the rules, there are two wills here. Christ *willed* to save them, as a hen wills to gather her chickens— the whole brood—but they *willed* not to be gathered. Would Christ, with sovereign will, desire to gather them, and then put in their minds the will not to be gathered? To affirm this would be an absurdity.

Whether it be Jacob, Esau, Pharaoh, Jews or Gentiles, none is predestinated without regard to the free acts of his own will. These texts they quote do not prove unconditional salvation. They do not rule out human willing as a condition for divine mercy. The *Rule of Unity* is an important principle of interpretation. We now use this rule on these words: "not of him that willeth"; and we shall see that the free choice of human will has always been required by God for His mercy and salvation.

God commanded that all Israel's worship, sacrifices and offerings had to be of their "free will." They offered unto the Lord "freewill offerings" (Lev. 22:18). This free-will offering was a "sweet savour unto the Lord" (Num. 15:3). This free-will offering is also specified in Deuteronomy 12:6; 23:23; II Chronicles 31:14. The worship of religious puppets would not be to God "a sweet savour."

When the Israelites brought their gifts to God, it was required that they come from "every man that giveth it *willingly* with his heart" (Ex. 25:2). It was repeatedly stated by Moses that a condition of acceptance for their offering was that it come from "whosoever is of a *willing* heart" (Ex. 35:5) — that it come from "every one whose heart stirred him up, and every one whom his spirit made willing" (Ex. 35:21). "As many as were willing hearted" brought offerings to the Lord (Ex. 35:22). (So also in Ex. 35:29.) "Accept, I beseech thee, the freewill offerings of my mouth, O Lord" (Ps. 119:108). These Old Testament saints knew that God would not accept a compelling or coercive worship. They knew that under God's gracious influence it was *their will, their* love, and *their* worship. Would this be required in Old Testament worship but not in New Testament worship?

> If ye be *willing* and obedient, ye shall eat the good of the land:
>
> But if ye refuse and rebel, ye shall be devoured with the sword. (Isa. 1:18, 19)

It was not a coercive obedience but willful obedience. God will accept no other worship. When Jesus said, "The true worshippers shall worship the Father in spirit and in truth . . . and they that worship him must worship him in spirit and in truth," did He not mean it was the true and willing spirit of the worshippers? Is not this implied in "*they* that worship him"? (John 4:23, 24).

"If any man *willeth* to do his will, he shall know of the teaching" (John 7:17, RV). Here Jesus clearly taught that the human will was a conditional factor in God's dealing with men. Seems to me that most of the controversy about the divine and human wills has been useless debate. The divine and human wills are distinctly set forth in many Scriptures as being separate. Each is presented as being something of its own.

"We love him, because he first loved us" (I John 4:19). God always does something *first*. He loved us, but it is also true that "*we* love him"—with our own love and our own wills. When the divine and human wills unite, eternal life is generated in the soul of the believer. All praise to God for His first part in our salvation, and no glory to man for his part. God gets there first, and when man is willing—the work is done. After Adam sinned, he didn't go searching for God, but God went looking for him. But I get the idea from the story that Adam was willing to be found.

The next part of the opposing argument in verse 16 uses the words: "nor of him that runneth, but of God that sheweth mercy." It is argued from this that our running has no part in our salvation. But this interpretation cannot stand up to the test of facts that we shall apply to it. These words do not mean that salvation is unconditional. They mean that men cannot originate nor earn their salvation by running—and that is all Paul intended them to mean. They do not rule out running as a condition.

Calvin and the Eternal Security interpreters use the important *Rule of Comparison* on other Bible doctrines, so we shall use it on this Scripture. We shall compare and interpret Paul in Romans by Paul in his other epistles.

The Structural Principles of the Bible, F. E. Marsh, is widely considered a "Bible Study Classic." On page 238, Marsh wrote:

> The careful comparison of one Scripture with another will generally explain a seeming contradiction.

Dean Alford, an eminent scholar, wrote:

> It should be a maxim for every expositor and every student, that Scripture is a *whole*, and stands or falls together.[18]

Leading Biblical and legal interpretation experts agree with this comparative rule. And if it is not allowed, then we cannot answer the critics who say: "The Bible is self-contradictory, and can be made to prove anything."

So we place in comparative position with Romans 9:16 other statements by Paul on running.

> Know ye not that they which run in a race run all, but one receiveth the prize? So run, that ye may obtain. . . .

> I therefore so run, not as uncertainly; so fight I, not as one that beateth the air. (I Cor. 9:24, 26)

> I have fought a good fight, I have finished my course [finished running the race], I have kept the faith:

> Henceforth there is laid up for me a crown of righteousness. (II Tim. 4:7, 8)

---

[18] *The New Testament for English Readers*, p. 29. Moody Press.

Paul told the Romans that God's mercy is not to him that runneth. But he told the Corinthians to run that they may obtain the prize. And he told Timothy, after he had finished the race, that the Lord would give him the victor's crown. In Hebrews, the Apostle told the people to run the race, and to lay aside every encumbrance that they might run it better.

Is there a contradiction between Paul in Romans and Paul in Corinthians and Timothy? Surely not. Different subjects were under consideration in these epistles. What was in Paul's mind in Romans is not what was in his mind in Corinthians and Timothy. It is required in interpretation that "language must be understood according to the subject-matter of discourse."

All the willing and running of man cannot save him. He cannot be his own savior. Without God's unmerited and unearned love and grace, no sinner can ever be saved, not even the heathen religious fanatics who torture themselves all their lives. But, God's free grace, undeserved as it is, did not dispense with *conditions* for man's salvation. Predestinating grace required faith, repentance, obedience, willing and running, as conditions. Further evidence of this will appear as we proceed.

The main thrust of the opposing argument in Romans 9 is in verses 19–24.

19. Thou wilt say then unto me. Why doth he yet find fault? For who hath resisted his will?

20. Nay but, O man, who art thou that repliest against God? Shall the thing formed say to him that formed it, Why hast thou made me thus?

21. Hath not the potter power over the clay, of the same lump to make one vessel unto honour, and another unto dishonour?

22. What if God, willing to shew his wrath, and to make his power known, endured with much longsuffering the vessels of wrath fitted to destruction:

23. And that he might make known the riches of his glory on the vessels of mercy, which he afore prepared unto glory,

24. Even us, whom he hath *called*, not of the Jews only, but also of the Gentiles?

The argument for Eternal Security from these verses goes like this: "As the potter is sovereign in forming vessels, so God is sovereign in forming moral agents. . . . He loves one and hates another. He exercises mercy toward some and hardens others, without reference to anything save His own sovereign will." [19]

It is fair to say that all Calvinists do not accept the above quotation. Semi-Calvinists do not agree with extreme Calvinists. Mr. Pink said that anyone who does not agree with his statement has "adulterated the truth." I will show you that the prophet Jeremiah adulterated it. Paul quoted the potter-clay verses from Jeremiah 18. But it was not within the purpose of Paul's thought to quote the context of the potter-clay verses. So we now go to Jeremiah and get the whole thought. *The Law of First Mention* can be of decisive importance in interpretation.

> The first mention of a thing, the very first words of any subject of which the Holy Spirit is going to treat, are the keystone of the whole matter.[20]

Let us now use this rule and you shall see that the Calvinist potter-clay argument is easily refuted by the context of Jeremiah 18.

---

[19] *The Sovereignty of God*, Arthur Pink, p. 111. 1930.
[20] *The Structural Principles of the Bible*, Marsh, F. E., p. 224. Kregel.

Then the word of the Lord came to me, saying,

O house of Israel, cannot I do with you as this potter? saith the Lord. Behold, as the clay is in the potter's hand, so are ye in mine hand, O house of Israel.

At what instant I shall speak concerning a nation, and concerning a kingdom, to pluck, and to pull down, and to destroy it;

If that nation, against whom I have pronounced, turn from their evil, I will repent of the evil that I thought to do unto them.

And at what instant I shall speak concerning a nation, and concerning a kingdom, to build and to plant it;

If it do evil in my sight, that it *obey* not my voice, then I will repent of the good, wherewith I said I would benefit them.

Now therefore go to, speak to the men of Judah, and to the inhabitants of Jerusalem, saying, Thus saith the Lord;

Behold, I frame evil against you, and devise a device against you: return ye now every one from his evil way, and make your ways and your doings good.

And they said, There is no hope: but we will walk after *our own* devices, and *we will* every one do the imagination of his evil heart. (Jer. 18: 5–12)

Here at the source of Paul's potter-clay quotation, the Potter pled with the Clay to repent of their evil and obey His voice. But the Clay, stubborn and rebellious, refused the Potter's offer of mercy and said they would walk in their own way and do the evil of their own hearts. The Potter twice used His if-condition to spare them the judgment soon to fall upon them. This Clay was not a lifeless thing. With its own spirit of rebellion, it rejected God's if-obey condition. Read the rest of God's conditional deal-

ings with them to the end of Jeremiah and you will
see why they were "vessels of wrath."

These facts should be sufficient to convince an
unprejudiced mind that in Romans 9 Paul was not
dealing with unconditional salvation. Now let us take
another look at Romans 9:22.

> What if God, willing to shew his wrath, and to
> make his power known, endured with much long-
> suffering the vessels of wrath fitted to destruc-
> tion.

This "willing" of God does not mean that the
Potter predestinated the Clay to be "vessels of
wrath." Dr. A. T. Robertson, top Greek authority,
wrote:

> Willing (thelon). Concessive use of the participle,
> "although willing," *not causal....* That they are
> responsible may be seen from I Thess. 2:15.[21]

Concerning this "fitted to destruction," Vine says
that Paul here speaks of "men persistent in evil,"
and that "fitted" is in "the Middle Voice, *indicating
that the vessels of wrath fitted themselves for destruction."* [22] (my emphasis)

On "vessel unto honour," we again use the *rule
of comparison* and get this:

> But in a great house there are not only vessels
> of gold and of silver, but also of wood and of
> earth; and some to honour and some to dishonour.
>
> *If* a man therefore purge himself from these, he
> shall be a *vessel unto honour,* sanctified, and
> meet for the master's use. (II Tim. 2:20, 21)

Vessel of honor is here connected with the conditional "if." To be such an honorable vessel it is

[21] *Word Pictures in the New Testament,* V. 4, p. 384.
[22] *Expository Dictionary of New Testament Words,* V. 1,
p. 304.

necessary that one *purge* himself from all that is displeasing to the Potter.

Follow Paul through the rest of Romans 9 and get his complete thought. Don't stop at verse 23 as Eternal Security expositors do, for in verses 30–33 he expands his thought and throws further light on the subject of the vessels of mercy and wrath.

30. What shall we say then? That the Gentiles, which follow not after righteousness, have attained to righteousness, even the righteousness of faith.

31. But Israel, which followed after the law of righteousness, hath not attained to the law of righteousness.

32. Wherefore? Because they sought it not by faith, but as it were by the works of the law. For they stumbled at that stumblingstone;

33. As it is written, Behold, I lay in Sion a stumblingstone and rock of offence: and whosoever believeth on him shall not be ashamed.

The words *faith* and *righteousness* stand large in these texts. The Gentile-clay "attained to righteousness, even the righteousness which is of faith." But Israel-clay did not attain to this righteousness. And Paul asks, "Wherefore?" Was it because they were predestinated not to attain to it? Paul answers: "Because they sought it not by faith. . . . *For* they stumbled at that stumblingstone." In their unbelief, they stumbled over Christ. To Gentile faith, Christ was the Stone. To Jewish unbelief, He was the Stumblingstone.

Paul extends this truth about Jews and Gentiles into chapters 10–11. The three chapters of Romans 9–10–11 are a Unit of Thought. Disregard the chapter divisions.

You cannot rightly understand Paul in these three chapters without this *unit of thought* principle.

There are many other sections of the Bible that you cannot understand without it. As it is applied to other doctrines, isn't it fair that it be applied to this one also? We now pick up the connecting link in chapter 10: 1–3:

1. Brethren, my heart's desire and prayer to God for Israel is, that they might be saved.

2. For I bear them record that they have a zeal for God, but not according to knowledge.

3. For they being ignorant of God's righteousness, and going about to establish *their own* righteousness, have not submitted themselves unto the righteousness of God.

It isn't necessary that anyone be a theologian to see from these verses that Israel, in establishing their own righteousness, refused God's righteousness which is by faith in Christ. The righteousness of God which is by faith in Christ is the center of the whole matter.

Israel refused to confess with their mouth the Lord Jesus Christ, and to believe in their heart that God had raised Him from the dead. Therefore, they could not be saved (v. 9). They had not "obeyed the gospel" (v. 16). God pled long with Israel, and "endured with much longsuffering" these vessels of wrath.

But to Israel he saith, All day long I have stretched forth my hands [pleading] unto a disobedient and gainsaying [contradicting] people. (Rom. 10: 21)

In chapter 11 we now see the last part of Paul's unit of thought about the Jews and Gentiles.

I say then, Hath God cast away his people? God forbid. For I also am an Israelite [he was a Christ-believer], of the seed of Abraham, of the tribe of Benjamin.

God hath not cast away his people which he
foreknew. Wot ye not what the Scripture saith of
Elias? how he maketh intercession to God against
Israel, saying,

Lord, they have killed thy prophets, and digged
down thine altars: and I am left alone, and they
seek my life.

But what saith the answer of God unto him? I
have reserved to myself seven thousand men, who
have not bowed the knee to the image of Baal.

Even so then at this present time also there is a
remnant according to the election of grace. (Rom.
11: 1–5)

Paul here dealt with questions about the Jewish
people. These questions were much discussed in
Paul's day, and serious meaning was attached to
them. Had God cast off His people the Jews? Paul's
answer was an emphatic no. He then referred back
to Jewish history. God always had a faithful "remnant" in Israel. Remnant means "A faithful and believing minority."

There was such a remnant in Elijah's day. Elijah,
during the apostasy of his time, thought he alone had
remained true to Jehovah's covenant. But God told
him there was a remnant of 7,000 in Israel who had
not bowed to the heathen Baal. It was through the
remnants that God fulfilled His covenant promise
to Abraham and David.

The remnant did not bow to Baal—when there
was powerful pressure upon them to do it. The
faithless majority yielded to this pressure and
bowed. God cast off the majority and "reserved"
the minority to himself. "God hath not cast away
his people [the remnant] which he *foreknew.*" God
foreknew they would not bow to Baal, and they are
His predestinated remnant "according to the election
of grace." Observe that "foreknew" and "election

of grace" are in a context about a remnant who were
faithful to God's covenant of salvation. The disobedient majority were not elected because they bowed
to Baal, killed God's prophets, and digged down
God's altars. God foreknew that too.

"Even so then at this present time also there is a
remnant." They refuse to bow to the "god of this
world." Sometimes the remnants are really small.
(There is much interesting truth in the Bible about
remnants for those who will study the subject.)

If the remnant of Elijah's time had bowed to
Baal, would they have been predestinated to God's
grace?

God has a faithful remnant in every generation.
They *could* bow to the gods of this world but they
will not. Faithfulness to God's covenant is a true
mark of every remnant. All God's elect have this
mark of identification. The non-elect do not.

Paul, in verses 17–24, extended the range of his
thought on the Jewish and Gentile questions raised
in chapters 9–10. Here he set forth the subject with
the symbol of an olive tree.

> And if some of the branches be broken off, and
> thou, being a wild olive tree, wert grafted in
> among them, and with them partakers of the root
> and fatness of the olive tree;
>
> Boast not against the branches. But if thou boast,
> thou bearest not the root, but the root thee.
>
> Thou wilt say then, The branches were broken off,
> that I might be grafted in.
>
> Well; *because of unbelief* they were broken off,
> and thou *standest by faith.* Be not highminded,
> but fear.
>
> For if God spared not the natural branches, take
> heed lest he also spare not thee.
>
> Behold therefore the goodness and severity of
> God: on them which fell, severity; but toward

thee, goodness, *if* thou *continue* in his goodness: otherwise thou also shalt be cut off.

And they also, *if* they abide not still in unbelief, shall be grafted in: for God is able to graft them in again.

Paul, greatest of theologians, stressed this if-condition in dealing with questions about God's purposes of salvation for Jews and Gentiles.

Paul taught that the Jewish branches were broken off their covenant tree "because of unbelief." The cause was Jewish unbelief—not a mysterious sovereign predestination. The Gentiles were grafted into the Jewish covenant tree because of their "faith." It was all a matter of faith and unbelief.

The specified if-condition lies deep in Paul's doctrine. The Jews would be grafted in again "*if* they abide not still in unbelief." And the Gentiles would also be broken off "if" they did not "continue" in faith. Jesus said: "*If* a man abide not in me, he is cast forth as a branch, and is withered . . . and they are burned" (John 15:6).

Here in Romans 11, Paul gave the if-condition its full force. As he made salvation conditional in chapter 11, it follows that he did not teach it was unconditional in chapter 9. There is salvation in God's covenant Tree for those who "*abide*" in it. Paul had no doctrine such as "once in the Tree, always in the Tree."

The evidence we have seen justifies our conclusion that God's foreknowledge is not causal. Foreordination is according to foreknowledge. "Jesus knew from the beginning who they were that believed not . . ." (John 6:64). God knew all things from the beginning and designed His eternal plans according to what He knew about men from the beginning. The words "predestination" and "election" in no way alter the fact that God formed His eternal plans for men according to what He foreknew they would do with their free power of decision.

John 2: 23–25 says that "many believed in his name, when they saw the miracles which he did. But Jesus did not commit himself unto them, because he knew all men, and needed not that any should testify of man: for he knew *what was in man.*" Jesus knew from the beginning *what* was in man. He knew the characters of men, whether they had faith or unbelief; whether they would accept or reject Him; whether they would continue in faith or be temporary believers like the "many" with a casual excitement about His miracles.

God, from the beginning, knew what was in Jacob, Esau, Pharaoh, and all of us. He is a "discerner of the thoughts and intents of the heart" (Heb. 4: 12). But these thoughts and intents are "what was in man."

Specialists working in the field of human behavior have developed a *predictive science* that is often amazingly accurate. After a character analysis, they often predict success in marriage or failure in business. Crime experts study the past record of a criminal and capture him by foreknowledge of his next move. Wars have been won by generals who knew the opposing general's habits of thought. We could go on down the line about school teachers and pupils, parents and children, husbands and wives, et cetera. How much more then does God know about human thoughts and intents and what is *in man?*

The interpretation of unconditional salvation from Romans 9 tramples over established interpretive laws. Our interpretation of conditional salvation from this chapter satisfies these laws. It would be a sad day for Christianity if other Bible doctrines had to be defended with the same method of interpretation that is used to defend Calvinistic predestination.

Our method does not pick and choose from a few texts in Romans 9 but reasons from Paul's complete unit of thought in the three chapters of 9–10–11. The if-evidence we saw in this unit overturns our opponent's conclusion drawn from a few selected verses in chapter 9. We could have presented further evidence from Romans. Example:

> For *if* ye live after the flesh, ye shall die: but *if* ye through the Spirit do mortify the deeds of the body, ye shall live.
>
> For *as many* as are *led* by the Spirit of God, *they* are the sons of God. (Rom. 8:13, 14)

Before leaving Romans let us consider another Eternal Security argument: "And so *all* Israel shall be saved: as it is written, There shall come out of Sion the Deliverer, and shall turn away ungodliness from Jacob" (Rom. 11:26). (Observe that they skipped over the *ifs* in verses 17–23 to get to verse 26.)

Their argument for unconditional salvation says that "all" Israel shall be saved. This is another distortion. Paul's statement is in a prophetic context. All Israel, the faithful remnant in the great tribulation, will be saved when the Deliverer comes out of Sion. Jesus refuted their argument when He told about the Israelite in "hell" forever. He also told about many other Israelites cast into "outer darkness" forever. "To whom is reserved the blackness of darkness forever" (Jude 6, 13; II Peter 2:17).

Salvation is of the Jews. Jesus and Paul taught that multitudes of Jews will be lost forever. The faithful "remnant" will be saved. These are God's predestinated ones whom He foreknew. They shall never be lost.

The if-evidence in Romans is convincing for conditional salvation. A proved fact is a proved fact,
and no amount of misinterpretation can make it
anything else. Let the reader examine the evidence.
There's always hope when people look fairly at all
sides.

10

The If-Condition in the

Epistles of Paul

FIRST CORINTHIANS

Before dealing with Paul's "if" in chapter 15:2, it may help our purpose to consider first one of the most important conditional passages in the New Testament. Note the flow of Paul's thought.

Know ye not that they which run in a race run all, but one receiveth the prize? So run, that ye may obtain.

And every man that striveth for the mastery is temperate in all things. Now they do it to obtain a corruptible crown; but we an incorruptible.

I therefore so run, not as uncertainly; so fight I, not as one that beateth the air:

But I keep under my body, and bring it into subjection: lest that by any means, when I have preached to others, I myself should be a castaway.

Moreover, brethren, I would not that ye should be ignorant, how that all our fathers were under the cloud, and all passed through the sea:

And were all baptized unto Moses in the cloud and in the sea;

And did all eat the same spiritual meat;

And did all drink the same spiritual drink; for
they drank of that spiritual Rock that followed
them: and that Rock was Christ.

But with many of them God was not well pleased:
for they were overthrown in the wilderness.

Now these things were our *examples,* to the intent
we should not lust after evil things, as they also
lusted.

Neither be ye idolaters, as were some of them;
as it is written, The people sat down to eat and
drink, and rose up to play.

Neither let us commit fornication, as some of them
committed, and fell in one day three and twenty
thousand. . . .

Now all these things happened unto them for *ensamples*: and they are written for our admonition,
upon whom the ends of the world are come.

Wherefore let him that thinketh he standeth take
heed lest he fall. (I Cor. 9: 24–27; 10: 1–12)

Does this passage teach conditional salvation?
Eternal Security teachers say it does not. Let us see
if we can learn its true meaning. First, it is necessary to see that these Scriptures are connected and
that they contain a complete thought. If this can
be proved, we shall win a major point for conditional
salvation.

Paul began his train of thought with an illustration from the Olympic games. Athletics was Paul's
favorite illustration in his Epistles. He used it more
than any other. He began with the footrace and referred to the strenuous training the athlete endured
to win the prize, which was a "corruptible crown."
In Paul's day, the Olympic athlete subjected himself
to 10 months of severe training for the games. If
the athlete broke the rules of the contest, he was
a "castaway," which meant *rejected.*

Paul said that he, as God's athlete, did not run

"uncertainly"; nor was he like one who "beateth the air." He said he kept his body under a severe discipline for fear that he be a castaway, like the athlete in his illustration. Paul, even with the "gift" of continence (I Cor. 7:7), and all the physical beatings and tortures he endured (II Cor. 11:23–27), spoke of his body as a strong power to be overcome and kept subdued. After all his preaching and labor for Christ he feared being a castaway. It will help much if we can prove the meaning of "castaway." We quote the highest authoritative sources.

On the meaning of "castaway" (*adokimos*), Professor A. T. Robertson, the "prince of modern Greek grammarians," wrote:

> It means not standing the test.... Paul means rejected for the *prize*, not for the entrance to the race. He will fail if he breaks the rules of the game (Matt. 7:22) .... Most writers take Paul to refer to the possibility of his rejection in his personal salvation at the end of the race.... At the end he has serene confidence (II Tim. 4:7) with the race run and won. It is a humbling thought for us all to see this wholesome fear instead of smug complacency in this greatest of all heralds of Christ.[1]

The new and highly authoritative *A Greek-English Lexicon of the New Testament*[2] says on page 18: "*Not standing the test,* then *unqualified, worthless, base ... disqualified.* I Cor. 9:27: *a man who is not tempted is unproved.*" (their italics). The combined weight of leading New Testament Greek authorities support the view that Paul referred to his salvation when he used the word "castaway" in I Corinthians 9:27.

---

[1] *Word Pictures in the New Testament*, V. 4, p. 150. Broadman Press, 1931.

[2] Arndt & Gingrich, University of Chicago Press, 1957.

Dean Alford, noted New Testament scholar, wrote that Paul feared he might be rejected from the prize, and not from the contest altogether, as some commentators make it, "for he was already *in it*." Then Alford added:

> An examination of the victorious combatants took place after the contest, and if it could be proved that they had contended unlawfully, or unfairly, they were deprived of the prize and driven with disgrace from the games. So the Apostle, if he had proclaimed the laws of the combat to others, and not observed them himself, however successful he might apparently be, would be personally rejected as unqualified in the great day.[3]

Vincent's Word Studies in the New Testament[4] says: "*Rejected,* as unworthy of the prize."

The *Amplified New Testament* has it: "I myself should become unfit—not stand the test and be unapproved—and rejected (as a counterfeit)."

This has the support of *The Vocabulary of the Greek New Testament.*[5] Greek scholars say this work is the "final court of appeals" on New Testament usage. There are many other supporting evidences.[6]

Read again the verses at the beginning of this chapter. I have disregarded the chapter division because it wasn't there when Paul wrote it. Now see

---

[3] *The New Testament for English Readers,* p. 1031. Moody Press.

[4] V. 3, p. 238. Eerdmans, 1957.

[5] Moulton & Milligan, p. 167. Eerdmans, 1959.

[6] *Thayer's Greek-English Lexicon of the New Testament,* p. 12.

The Expositors Greek Testament, V. 2, p. 857.

Vine's Expository Dictionary of New Testament Words, V. 1, p. 173.

Trench's Synonyms of the New Testament, pp. 278–279.

Manual Greek Lexicon of the New Testament, Abbott-Smith, p. 10.

The International Standard Bible Encyclopedia, V. 1, p. 582.

how Paul develops his thought. He told about running the race to obtain the prize. Then, referring to his salvation, he told about his self-denial and rigid bodily discipline. He said he did this because he did not want the great Judge to disqualify him in the end as a castaway, or as one unworthy of the prize. The Olympic contestant was examined by the judges after the race before receiving the prize. This often happens today. A fighter's purse is held up; winners are stripped of their medals; and others have been banished for life from further participation in athletic contests because they broke the rules. While I write these pages there comes news of a cheating scandal at our Air Force Academy in Colorado. Thirty football players and many others were forced to resign from the Academy because they broke the rules. This often happens in other colleges. There are star athletes disgraced and banished for life for the same reason. They are *castaways*.

This is what Paul feared would happen to him at the Judgment. He would not let the power of sin get its mastery over him. Any uncertainty of reaching the goal for the prize was not distrust of God but distrust of himself. He was sure that God is able to keep that which he had committed unto Him, and in the sure-footed certainty of God's faithfulness he moved with exerted effort toward the prize.

Next, in the movement of Paul's thought, watch as he goes from "castaway" to "moreover":

> ...lest that by any means, when I have preached to others, I myself should be a castaway.

> *Moreover,* brethren, I would not that ye should be ignorant, how that all our fathers were under the cloud, and all passed through the sea. (I Cor. 9: 27; 10: 1)

This connective, "moreover," proves there is here a *unit of thought.* Paul thus gives us "ensamples" of what he meant by castaway. Leading Greek authorities agree that the full meaning of castaway is expressed in the connective force of "moreover." The famous Baptist scholar, Professor A. T. Robertson, wrote:

> Moreover *(for)*. Paul appeals to the experience of the Israelites in the wilderness in confirmation of his statement concerning himself in 9:26, and as a powerful warning to the Corinthians.[7]

> Moreover *(for)* . . . introducing an illustration of rejection by God, and thus connecting what follows with the close of the last chapter. It is possible that I may be rejected, *for* the Israelites were.[8]

> Moreover *(for)*. It serves to explain, make clear, illustrate, a preceding thought or word: *for*, that is, *namely;* so that it begins an exposition of the thing just announced.[9]

> *Moreover* (for) . . . a conjunction used to express cause, inference, *continuation, or to explain.*[10] (my italics)

The *Expositors Greek Testament* is an authoritative work by 17 distinguished Greek scholars. In Volume 2, page 857, it says of this "moreover" in relation to "castaway":

> The Apostle has just confessed in warning others, his own fear of reprobation. That this is no idle fear the history of the Old Testament plainly proves. All the Israelite fathers were rescued from Egypt, and sealed with the ancient sacraments, and virtually partook of Christ in the wilderness; but, alas, how few of those first redeemed entered the Promised Land!

---

[7] *Word Pictures in the New Testament*, V. 4, p. 151.

[8] *Vincent's Word Studies in the New Testament*, V. 3, p. 238.

[9] *Thayer's Greek-English Lexicon of the New Testament*, p. 110.

[10] *A Greek-English Lexicon of the New Testament*, Arndt & Gingrich, p. 151.

The reader can further verify the meaning of "moreover" (Gr. *gar*) in *The Vocabulary of the Greek New Testament,* Moulton & Milligan, page 121; *A Manual Greek Lexicon of the New Testament,* Abbott-Smith, page 88.

Paul said the Scriptures about Israel's "ensamples" were written "for our admonition." The Israelites were tested and rejected. This is the whole point of Paul's warning about "castaway." There is much in the Bible about God's testing and proving His people. God *proves* that He might *approve.* That which is genuine passes the test, but the counterfeit breaks down under the test. The illustration of the testing of coins and metals in relation to Christians has considerable importance in the Bible. An example is I Peter 1: 7. Christians may sometimes fail in a test but it is the exception and not the rule. This was true of Abraham and David.

God proved the Israelites many times before rejecting them. He brought them to the bitter waters of Marah, "and there he proved them." They murmured against God and Moses. When they desired the fleshpots of Egypt, God said He would "prove them, whether they will walk in my law, or no." Moses told them at Sinai: "God is come to prove you." He also told them that God led them for 40 years in the wilderness "to prove thee, to know what was in thine heart, whether thou wouldest keep his commandments, or no." (Ex. 15: 25; 16: 4; 20: 20; Deut. 8: 2; Judg. 2: 22).

Paul emphasized that the Israelites were tested through fleshly desires and pleasures. They "lusted . . . sat down to eat and drink, and rose up to play"; and they committed fornication. Satan has more success with these temptations than with anything else.

Paul told these Corinthians, *"Examine* yourselves, whether ye be in the faith; *prove* your own selves. Know ye not your own selves, how that Jesus

Christ is in you, except ye be reprobates [counterfeits]?" (II Cor. 13:5).

In "examine" and "prove" there is the idea of *proving* to determine whether persons are worthy to be accepted or not. Those that endure the proving are accepted as genuine, and those that do not are rejected as counterfeit. This was true of Israelites in the wilderness provings. Those who failed the testings were rejected as counterfeits. Jeremiah said the Jews in his time were counterfeits. "Reprobate [counterfeit] silver shall men call them, because the Lord hath rejected them" (Jer. 6:30). They were castaways.

God tests everyone. All must be proved to determine if they are worthy to enter the Kingdom of God. Paul told the Corinthians to test themselves—as metals are tested—to see whether they "be in the faith." If they were reprobates, Christ was not in them, because Christ is not in counterfeits. Here are the opinions of two high ranking Greek authorities for Paul's truth about reprobates:

> *Unless indeed ye be reprobate....* Paul challenged his opposers in Corinth to try themselves, to test themselves, whether they were "in the faith."... Such tests can be made, unless, alas, they are "reprobate" (adokmoi), the very adjective that Paul held up before himself as a dreadful outcome to be avoided, I Cor. 9:27.[11]

> ...the falsehearted and those who belong to God only in semblance and in show...being proved or tempted, they will *appear* to be what they have always *been*.[12] (his italics)

Some Calvinist writers make Paul's "castaway" to mean: "To put on the shelf." Cracked pots were

---

[11] *Word Pictures in the New Testament*, A. T. Robertson, V. 4, p. 270.

[12] *Synonyms of the New Testament*, Trench, R. C., p. 279. Eerdmans, 1958.

put on the shelf, and Paul did not want to be a cracked pot on the shelf. These writers give no proof for this because they have none, and it is easy to refute: Paul's "ensamples" from Israel's apostate history were not cracked pots on the shelf. They were evil covenant breakers whose carcasses fell in the desert and who shall never enter God's rest.

Greek professor Kenneth Wuest, of Moody Bible Institute, translated "castaway" like this: "lest . . . I myself should be disqualified (from further Christian service)." [13] This is not a true translation.

In the Appendix of this book there are listed eight world-wide adopted rules of interpretation. In the *rule of definition* I quoted Professor Wuest: "The content of meaning in these words is not to be determined by each individual expositor . . . to do so would be a method of interpretation (that is) a most vicious thing."

It surely is a most vicious thing. The false teaching in Christian Science, Jehovah's Witnesses, Unity, Higher Liberalism, and many others is the result of this most vicious thing. "Sin," as defined by Mrs. Eddy, is an "illusion." To Fosdick, "damnation" is "that old hell" that no intelligent person can believe. "Born again" is stripped of all its glory by some. With others, "everlasting life" means what these words mean but "everlasting punishment" does not, and so on down the line. They are all dangerous distortions of Bible words.

Professor John H. Wigmore, one of America's famous legal authorities, wrote about this vicious method of interpretation in his textbook, *Wigmore on Evidence*.[14] Professor Wigmore called some in-

---

[13] *Wuest's Expanded Translation of the Greek New Testament*, V. 2, p. 154. Eerdmans, 1958. (Used by permission.)
[14] Pages 521–529. Foundation Press, Inc. 1935.

terpreters "word-magicians," and said that if these interpreters can make words mean what they want them to mean, then there is no need for rules of interpretation. He then asks: "What is the *standard* of interpretation?" "In what *sources* is the standard to be found?" And on page 523, he has the *Rule Against Disturbing a Plain Meaning.*

I have quoted leading legal authorities because in this book we have based our arguments on God's covenants, and covenants are legal transactions. Therefore, the same interpretive laws that apply to other covenants also apply to God's covenants.

Search the history of false doctrines and you will find these word-magicians everywhere. To prove the meaning of "castaway" we quoted ten Greek works holding the highest authoritative positions. They are *standard sources of evidence.* We proved the meaning by the *rule of definition,* and by the *rule of context,* and by the *rule of usage* and also by other rules in the Appendix. Our interpretation satisfies all the rules. Professor Wuest's translation violates them all.

Dr. James Moffatt , translator of *Moffatt's Translation of the Holy Bible,* wrote this about "castaway" in I Corinthians 9:27:

> [Castaway] "conveys a serious idea...this is borne out by the following warning, (10:1–11...the latter illustration from Israel with the desert sacraments broadens the range of *disqualified.* To be *disqualified* is the opposite of securing one's share in the final salvation.... The whole context and illustration is about salvation.[15]

John Calvin wrote concerning this passage:

> Paul says...there is no point of difference between the Israelites and us, which would put our

---

[15] *The First Epistle to the Corinthians,* p. 127–128, James Moffatt.

whole situation in a different category from theirs. Therefore, because he [Paul] intended to threaten the Corinthians with the same vengeance which befell the Israelites. . . . [Paul said] Therefore, you should be afraid, because the same thing threatens you. Jude uses the same argument in his letter.[16]

Going now to I Corinthians 15: 1–2, we read:

Moreover, brethren, I declare unto you the gospel which I preached unto you, which also ye have received, and wherein ye stand;

By which also ye are saved, *if* ye keep in memory what I preached unto you, unless ye have believed in vain.

Here "if" carries the same conditional force as all the other ifs we have seen. "The salvation of the readers depends on their holding fast the word preached" (*Vincent's Word Studies*).

The Greek text reads here: ". . . the gospel . . . by which *ye are being saved." The Expositors Greek Testament* says: "saved (sozesthe) affirms a *present, continuous* salvation, cf. Rom. 8: 24; Eph. 2: 8." Dr. Robertson in his *Word Pictures in the New Testament* wrote: "Condition of first class. . . . Paul holds this peril over them in their temptation to deny the resurrection."

On this "believed in vain," Dr. James Moffatt wrote in his commentary on First Corinthians that Paul said we are not saved " 'by random impulse.' Paul calls it 'futile make-believe' . . . 'light half-believers.' " And John Calvin in his commentary on this verse, wrote: "*If ye hold fast, except ye believed in vain.* These two conditional clauses have a sharp sting in them." So, in this Scripture we see

---

[16] *Calvin's Commentaries*, The First Epistle of Paul to the Corinthians, p. 200, Editors, D. W. Torrance, T. F. Torrance; Oliver & Boyd, London, 1960.

another condition for salvation: We must believe Bible doctrines—as taught by Paul.

It isn't necessary to deal with all Paul's ifs, but we quote two or three more before passing to other Epistles.

> And you...hath he reconciled...to *present* you holy and unblameable and unreproveable in his sight:
>
> *If* ye continue in the faith grounded and settled, and be not moved away from the hope of the gospel. (Col. 1: 21–23)

The Greek text expresses a continuous process. The Colossians would be presented to the Lord in holiness provided they continued in the faith. That is the only way the holiness could be accomplished. Holiness, or sanctification, is a major Bible doctrine and is given much importance in relation to salvation, as you can see in these texts. The Holy Spirit is grieved that this truth is largely neglected by ministers and Christians today. Notice this "present" in other texts:

> For I am jealous over you with godly jealousy: for I have espoused you to one husband, that I may *present* you as a chaste virgin to Christ. (II Cor. 11: 2)
>
> Christ also loved the church, and gave himself for it;
>
> That he might sanctify and cleanse it with the washing of water by the word,
>
> That he might *present* it to himself a glorious church. (Eph. 5: 25–27)
>
> Whom we preach, warning every man, and teaching every man in all wisdom; that we may *present* every man perfect in Christ Jesus. (Col. 1: 28)
>
> Now unto him that is able to keep you from falling, and to *present* you faultless before the presence of his glory with exceeding joy. (Jude 24)

Paul, in Ephesians 1:4, 5, has holiness connected with predestination.

> According as he hath chosen us in him before the foundation of the world, that we should be holy and without blame before him in love:
>
> Having predestinated us unto the adoption of children by Jesus Christ to himself, according to the good pleasure of his will.

"Chosen . . . that we should be holy . . . without blame . . . in love . . . predestinated . . . good pleasure of his will." If you pluck "predestinated" out of these texts and detach it from "holy without blame . . . in love," you have a distortion. Predestination does not stand alone in the Scriptures. It has conditional connections. If it is disconnected from some of its conditions, why not also disconnect it from the conditions of "repent and believe"?

Chosen to be holy and without blame was part of the predestinated plan. When God determined the end, He also determined the means to reach the end. Paul's Jewish "ensamples" were chosen to be "a peculiar people unto himself" (Deut. 1:2), but they became lustful and disobedient and did not reach the Promised Land—the covenant objective—because they violated the conditions necessary to reach the objective.

God chose His people—picked them out—to be His adopted children in Christ. Without the Calvary-Christ, there is no election. They were picked out to be holy and blameless. This was the "good pleasure of his will"—His sovereign will. These predestination truths stand in strong opposition to the predestination teaching which says that God had made special provision to save those who continue in sin. Paul told the Colossians the sovereign will and purpose would be accomplished *"if* ye continue in the faith . . . and be not moved away from the gospel."

Paul has another "if" in I Timothy 5: 8. Some who professed salvation had neglected to provide for their families and parents. Paul said:

> But *if* any provide not for his own, and specially those of his own house, he hath denied the faith, and is worse than an infidel.

We have seen some who claim salvation, with fine homes and good salaries, push off their aged parents on others for care. And it has been sickening to hear these and others say, when told of their Scriptural responsibilities: "We are saved by faith, not by works." Claim what they will, Paul said they are worse than infidels.

In I Timothy 4: 16, Paul told Timothy to do something for his salvation and the salvation of others.

> Take heed unto thyself, and unto the doctrine; *continue* in them: for in *doing* this thou shalt both save thyself, and them that hear thee.

It was by continuing in the doctrines of Christ and by doing them that Timothy and his hearers would be saved. We agree with Calvin's comment on this text:

> True, it is God alone that saves; and not even the smallest portion of his glory can lawfully be bestowed on men. But God parts with no portion of his glory when he employs the agency of men for bestowing salvation.[17]

Salvation is of the Jews. But Paul warned the Corinthians of Jews who were not saved. "The people sat down to eat and drink, and rose up to play." They were "castaways." Paul, a Jew, said he brought his body under subjection to God's conditions for

---

[17] *Commentary on the First Epistle of Timothy*, John Calvin, p. 118. Eerdmans, 1948.

salvation. He said the Jewish castaways are our "ensamples," and the history of their lustings was written for "our admonition." Paul obeyed God's salvation conditions to avoid the dreaded end of being a castaway.

The Jews Paul warned about would not have been castaways if they had done what Paul did. Two of the original number—Joshua and Caleb— were not castaways. God had a remnant of two. Out of a 40-year massive covenant operation, God had two men who had "wholly followed the Lord." They had fulfilled the covenant condition to reach the covenant objective. The condition was to wholly follow the Lord. God said: "Surely none of the men that came up out of Egypt ... shall see the land which I sware unto Abraham ... because they have not wholly followed me: save Caleb ... and Joshua ... for they have wholly followed the Lord" (Num. 32: 11, 12).

11

The If-Condition in the

Hebrews Epistle

> Therefore we ought to give the more earnest heed
> to the things which we have heard, lest at any time
> we should let them slip.
>
> For if the word spoken by angels was stedfast, and
> every transgression and disobedience received a
> just recompence of reward;
>
> How shall we escape, *if* we neglect so great sal-
> vation; which at the first began to be spoken by
> the Lord, and was confirmed unto us by them that
> heard him? (Heb. 2:1–3)

THE APOSTLE SAID that if we do not give diligent
attention to the Gospel we have heard, we let these
saving truths slip away from us. Mosaic law punished every disobedience with a just penalty. How
then shall we escape if we neglect so great salvation?

This salvation is so great because God's great
love provided it, and a great Saviour paid a great
price for it. Therefore, he who neglects it has a
great guilt and will receive a great punishment. The
guilt and punishment will be in proportion to the
greatness of the salvation.

The Apostle appealed to the history of covenant-breaking Israel. Every transgression of Mosaic covenant law was punished. This warning of Israel's covenant disobedience is scattered many times throughout the Scriptures. And it proves that New Covenant lawbreakers shall likewise receive not only an eternal covenant penalty—but a "sorer punishment" (Heb. 10:29). This fact alone condemns the teaching of unconditional salvation.

How shall we escape? The question expresses denial. There is no escape from the penalties of covenant disobedience, as there was none under Moses. Escape is impossible. He who persists in sin, persists in an evil course of condemnation. He tramples over the covenant blood of Christ and rushes to his eternal doom.

The Apostle's next "if" is in Hebrews 3:6, 14:

> But Christ as a son over his own house; whose house are we, *if* we hold fast the confidence and the rejoicing of the hope firm *unto the end.*

> For we are made partakers of Christ, *if* we hold the *beginning* of our confidence stedfast *unto the end.*

To be a member of "the household of God" (Eph. 2:19), *one must remain in the House.* He must continue in faith and hope "unto the end." Observe, "the beginning . . . unto the end." Genuine faith will meet all enemies and conquer them; but counterfeit faith is conquered by enemies. Temporary faith "dureth for a while" (Matt. 13:21); but genuine faith "endureth to the end" (Matt. 10:22). He must not only believe, he must believe unto the end. He must not only overcome, he must overcome unto the end. Professor A. T. Robertson, in his commentary on verse 14, quoted Jonathan Edwards, the famous Calvinist theologian: "Jonathan Edwards once said that the sure proof of election is that one holds out to the end."

> If the Bible teaches the final perseverance of the
> saints, it also teaches that the saints are those who
> finally persevere in Christ. Continuance is the
> test of reality. . . . And indeed, to hold fast to
> hope is throughout the New Testament an indis-
> pensable condition of attaining the goal of full
> salvation.[1]

In Hebrews, as in many other Scriptures, the if-
warnings in relation to faithless Israel are constantly
held before our view. Chosen as they were to be
God's covenant people, their lustings and cravings
led them to unbelief and death. Their burial place
was named kibroth-hattaavah, meaning, "graves of
lust," because "there they buried the people that
lusted" (Num. 11:34). Thousands today who live
and persist in such unlawful indulgences have an
unshakeable belief that they are eternally predestinated for salvation. They worship the money-god,
the pleasure-god, the sex-god, and believe that God
has made a special provision for them so that they
can never be lost. Satan has no greater deception.
    Consider another if-warning:

> For as touching those who were once enlightened
> and tasted of the heavenly gift, and were made par-
> takers of the Holy Spirit and tasted the good word
> of God, and the powers of the age to come, and
> then fell away, it is impossible to renew them
> again unto repentance; seeing they crucify to them-
> selves the Son of God afresh, and put him to an
> open shame. For the land which hath drunk the
> rain that cometh oft upon it, and bringeth forth
> herbs meet for them for whose sake it is also
> tilled, receiveth blessing from God; but *if* it bear-
> eth thorns and thistles, it is rejected and nigh unto
> a curse; whose end is to be burned. (6:4–8, RV)

Some Calvinists admit that this Scripture has
stopped them on unconditional salvation. And all the

---

[1] *The New International Commentary on the New Testament*,
p. 213. Eerdmans, 1957.

language-twisting and word-magic of others leave the facts unexplained. "Facts are stubborn things." Their explanations do not explain "impossible," "fall away," and "renew them again." The *Pulpit Commentary* says: "Calvin's predestinarian views compelled him and his followers to do violence to the plain meaning of the passage."

The Apostle speaks of those who were "once enlightened ... tasted of the heavenly gift ... made partakers of the Holy Ghost ... tasted the good word of God, and the powers of the world to come." Robertson's *Word Pictures* and the *Expositors Greek Testament* say that these were actual spiritual experiences enjoyed by these people. Does God give such experiences to *unsaved* people?

It was impossible to "renew them *again*" if they fell away. So, *they had been regenerated and renewed before*. The authority of Greek grammar supports this statement.

The Apostle bluntly stated the impossibility of renewal for such people. "Such falling away after such experience precludes the possibility of repentance. On such persons the powers of grace have been exhausted" (*Pulpit Commentary*).

Then the Apostle used an illustration from nature. The earth that brings forth good fruit receives blessing; that which brings forth thorns and briars is rejected, and is nigh unto cursing; whose end is to be burned. The word "rejected" here means "castaway" (Gr. *adokimos*), and it is the same word that Paul used in I Corinthians 9:27 when he said he feared being a castaway (rejected, *adokimos*). The thorns and briars were not "put on the shelf"; they were "nigh unto cursing," and will be "burned."

Those who had received the spiritual experiences described by the Apostle were two classes of people. Both had received the "rain that cometh oft upon it." One class brought forth fruit that receiveth blessing. The other brought forth thorns and briars that were nigh unto cursing. "The contrast is between two classes of *Christians* under equally favorable conditions, out of which they develop opposite results" (*Vincent's Word Studies*).

Some expositors say this warning was for those Jewish Christians who were tempted to return to Judaism and escape persecution for being Christians. But the warnings in Hebrews cannot be limited to that. The Apostle repeatedly admonished them with the "ensamples" from Jewish history, and they were destroyed because of their sinful indulgences.

Jesus said we could know them "by their fruits," which means that we can know them by their "thorns and briars." The famous Baptist scholar, A. T. Robertson, in his commentary on this passage wrote: "It is a terrible picture and cannot be toned down."

The Apostle knew the Christians to whom he wrote, and said in verse 9 that he was "persuaded better things" of them; but the experience he described had happened to others. We wish we could be so persuaded of many thorns-and-briars believers, for when we give them God's oft-repeated if-warnings, they say with offended spirit: "Are you trying to get me to doubt my salvation?"

The class of professing Christians described here should not be confused with the ordinary backslider. A few of these do return to God and are restored. David and Peter sinned, but sin was the exception in their lives. If they had *persisted* in those sins, the story would be different.

In chapter 8: 8, 9, the Apostle again reminded his readers of the Hebrew covenant-breakers under Moses:

> Behold, the days come, saith the Lord, when I will make a new covenant with the house of Israel and with the house of Judah:

> Not according to the covenant that I made with
> their fathers when I took them by the hand to lead
> them out of the land of Egypt; because they con-
> tinued not in my covenant, and I regarded them
> not, saith the Lord.

This Scripture was quoted from Jeremiah 31:31–34, which has the detail: ". . . my covenant they brake, *although I was an husband unto them,* saith the Lord." God's covenant with Israel was a *covenant of wedlock.* There is much truth in the Bible on this subject.

This Jehovah-Husband Israel-Wife relationship was conditional, as it was between Israelites. Un-faithfulness to the nuptial tie was always a major offense in the family life of the nation and was pun-ishable by death from the beginning as seen in Genesis 38:24. Under Mosaic covenant law, adultery was a "sin unto death." "The adulterer and adulter-ess shall surely be put to death"—"so shalt thou put away evil from Israel" (Lev. 20:10; Deut. 22:22). To profane God's holy covenant of matrimony was a crime so shocking that Jehovah demanded the death penalty. The guilty were "cut off" from the innocent and from the covenant nation in the inter-ests of the Hebrew State.

There are numerous references in Jeremiah, Ezekiel, and Hosea that speak of this Husband-Wife relationship between Jehovah and Israel. Israel was Jehovah's harlot wife. When Israel-Wife "played the harlot with many lovers" (Jer. 2:20; 3:1), Jehovah-Husband forgave and invited her to return. This she refused to do and continued in her harlotries. Jeho-vah was a "jealous" Husband—"whose name is Jealous" (Ex. 20:5; 34:14). The Divine Lover, after long patience, carried out His threats. In jealous vengeance, He poured out His wrath upon the adul-terous nation. The merciless slaughter, the captiv-ities, and the plunder of her country by heathen armies bear impressive witness to the awfulness of the penalty she suffered for violations of her wedlock.

"They continued not in my covenant, and I regarded them not." In legal language such a covenant is known to this day as a *Continuing Covenant.*[2] Such a covenant indicates the successive performance of specific acts as embodied in the covenant. A *breach of covenant* nullifies its provisions. "The Israelites broke the covenant. Then God annulled it. . . . The covenant was void when they broke it" (Robertson).

Some Eternal Security teachers quote Jeremiah 3:14 to confirm their unconditional salvation: "Turn, O backsliding children, saith the Lord; for I am married unto you." But they don't quote other Jeremiah passages and Hebrews 8:9, which show that God cast them off when they did not return.

Isaiah called Jerusalem the "harlot city" (1:21). When Jesus wept over this Harlot, He announced the awful doom of that "adulterous generation" which was fulfilled under the Roman general Titus in 70 A.D. Jesus gave details about what Titus would do when he destroyed the city: "Thine enemies shall cast a trench about thee, and compass thee round, and keep thee in on every side . . . shall lay thee even with the ground, and thy children within thee . . . not leave in thee one stone upon another" (Luke 19:41–44).

The "house" of Israel would be left to them "desolate." Their covenant protection would be withdrawn. Jehovah-Husband would no longer live with the Harlot.

Josephus, the Jewish historian, wrote a graphic

---

[2] See *Black's Law Dictionary*, p. 437. 4th edition; West Pub. Co., 1957.

record of the fulfillment of Christ's prophecy. When Titus besieged the city, the Jews' supplies were reduced until they ate from sewers and dunghills. No persuasion from Titus or Josephus could induce them to surrender to save their lives. They cut the throats of family members who talked peace. Those who tried to desert to the Romans were slaughtered by their kindred.

Titus desired to save the city and temple, but the insane refusal of the Jews to surrender caused the soldiers to murder them until they wearied of the killing. There were 1,100,000 slain. And 600,000 dead bodies were thrown out at the gates and piled in heaps. They had crucified their Covenant-Messiah, and the Romans crucified them until there was no place to put the crosses. Others in suicidal frenzy leaped from the wall and were crushed to death. The frightful terror and unparalleled cruelty did not spare the aged and infants. Josephus wept and Titus groaned at the ghastly horror. Condemned and doomed, centuries of accumulated wrath had "come upon them to the uttermost" (Matt. 23:35; I Thess. 2:16). "Whenever iniquity has reached its last stage, the judgment of heaven is at hand" (Fairbarn).

They had despised the Prophet of Nazareth but believed the false prophets who seduced them with promises of a miraculous deliverance. In the end they saw they were deceived and killed themselves in frantic madness. Others were taken as slaves. Josephus wrote:

> Thus there was a star resembling a sword, which stood over the city, and a comet, that continued a whole year.[3]

The divine sword devoured them. The full fury of the covenant curse fell upon them, as the true

---

[3] *Josephus Historical Works*, H. T. Coates Co., p. 824.

prophets had warned, but which the false prophets said would never happen because they were God's chosen and elected nation.

God's sword of vengeance has slashed the Harlot through 19 centuries. In our time we have seen the savagery of Hitler's colossal massacre of six million of them, and the worst is yet to come (Luke 21: 20–24). The Jewish State has been restored and Jews are returning there, but the full force of God's vengeance and wrath upon the covenant-breakers has yet to fall upon them.

There is a point in God's dealings with sinners when He gives up. "God gave them up" (Rom. 1: 24–26). The Jews had rejected repeated warnings:

> For *if* we sin wilfully after that we have received the knowledge of the truth, there remaineth no more sacrifice for sins.
>
> But a certain fearful looking for of judgment and fiery indignation, which shall devour the adversaries.
>
> He that despised Moses' law died without mercy under two or three witnesses:
>
> Of how much sorer punishment, suppose ye, shall he be thought worthy, who hath trodden under foot the Son of God, and hath counted the *blood of the covenant,* wherewith he was sanctified, an unholy thing, and hath done despite unto the Spirit of grace?
>
> For we know him that hath said, Vengeance belongeth unto me, I will recompense, saith the Lord. And again, The Lord shall judge his people.
>
> It is a fearful thing to fall into the hands of the living God. (Heb. 10: 26–31)

We have seen that under Moses there was no sacrifice for willful and persistent sin. This is true under both covenants. God's love and mercy are great, but He has set a limit. As we saw in the Old

Covenant, the deliberate sinner had to bear his own guilt. The covenant sacrifice could not atone for him. Persistent sinning against the "knowledge of the truth" leads one to a hopeless state. He passes to a state from which there is no recovery. Every divine means for his salvation has been exhausted.

The Apostle referred to those who had persisted in deliberate sin and had trampled over the covenant blood of Christ wherewith he was sanctified. They were not only saved but had advanced to the position of sanctification. Their guilt involved them in the "blood of the covenant." They had insulted the Holy Spirit.

This Apostle threatened them again and again. Warnings were repeated: "fearful judgment," "fiery indignation," "sorer punishment," "fearful thing," "devour," "vengeance." How come that many who preach so much about the love of God never get around to these truths?

"Willful sin, continued in, means apostasy, repudiation of the covenant" (*Expositors Greek Testament*). "Such a covenant-breaking people could no longer be the subject of covenant mercy on God's part" (Delitzsch, *Commentary on Hebrews*).

We go on to chapter 12: 7, 8:

> *If* ye *endure* chastening, God dealeth with you as with sons; for what son is he whom the father chasteneth not?

> But *if* ye be without chastisement, whereof all are partakers, then are ye bastards, and not sons.

The Apostle's blunt language jolts us to the reality of the facts. There were two classes of people in the first-century churches, as in the twentieth-century churches: those who endured God's chastenings and those who did not. Those who endured the chastenings were God's sons. Those who did not

were bastards. Endurance was evidence of divine
sonship. Non-endurance was proof of bastardy. The
genuine and counterfeit are again revealed for what
they are by a test—an *endurance test.*

Abraham received the promise "after he had pa-
tiently endured" (Heb. 6:15). Moses "endured, as
seeing him who is invisible" (Heb. 11:27). Christ
"endured the cross" (Heb. 12:2). Those who "have
no root in themselves ... *endure but for a time*"
(Mark 4:17). My Greek New Testament has this
verse: "*they* are *temporary.*" Endurance is the greatest test.

It is evident the Hebrews were beset with various dangers. Some were tempted to deny Christ to
avoid persecution. To others tempted with lusts,
there went the Esau-warning: "looking diligently
. . . lest there be any fornicator or profane person,
as Esau." For others there was the root-of-bitterness
warning (Heb. 12:15). The deadliness of each sin
was like a serpent's fangs. A man dead with infec-
tion is as dead as one with a heart attack.

> Now the just shall live by faith: but *if* any man
> draw back, my soul shall have no pleasure in him.
>
> But we are not of them that draw back unto per-
> dition; but of them that believe to the saving of
> the soul. (Heb. 10:38–39)

The just live by faith in Christ—continuously.
They do not draw back. Those who draw back, go
back unto perdition. They go back to this perdition
because they do not endure; they do not continue
to live in Christ by faith. When one draws back
unto perdition, it is evident that he is not elected to
salvation because with freedom of decision he chose
perdition. He does not continue in Christ. He continues in sin.

Jesus said: "My sheep ... follow me"—continuously. They do not draw back to sin. They could but won't. These are the ones of whom Jesus said: "No man is able to pluck them out of my Father's hand" (John 10:27–29). The others are not in the Father's hand because they turn back from Christ and continue in sin. This is perdition. To endure in Christ is to "believe to the saving of the soul."

Salvation is of the Jews. But those who draw back do not share in this salvation. This Epistle, like others, used the ancient Israelites as warnings. Once in the Covenant, and sustained by God's mighty miracles of salvation, yet, under God's covenant curse, they rotted in "graves of lust."

> Wherefore (as the Holy Ghost saith, To day if ye will hear his voice,
>
> Harden not your hearts, as in the provocation, in the day of temptation in the wilderness:
>
> When your fathers tempted me, proved me, and saw my works forty years.
>
> Wherefore I was grieved with that generation, and said, They do alway err in their heart; and they have not known my ways.
>
> So I sware in my wrath, They shall not enter into my rest.)
>
> Take heed, brethren, lest there be in any of you an evil heart of unbelief, in departing from the living God.
>
> But exhort one another daily, while it is called To day; lest any of you be hardened through the deceitfulness of sin. (Heb. 3:7–13)

Let us obey the Apostle's exhortation to "run with patience the race that is set before us .... Looking unto Jesus" (Heb. 12:1, 2). Like Paul, God's great spiritual athlete, let us press onward to the prize; ever onward to the Goal Post with our eyes

continually fixed upon Jesus. Do this, dear reader,
and you will be predestinated to eternal salvation.

> Blessed is the man that *endureth* temptation: for
> *when* he is tried, he shall receive the crown of
> life, which the Lord hath promised to them that
> love him. (James 1: 12)

The If-Condition in the

General Epistles

JAMES

But be ye doers of the word, and not hearers only, deceiving your own selves.

For *if* any be a hearer of the word, and not a doer, he is like unto a man beholding his natural face in a glass:

For he beholdeth himself, and goeth his way, and straightway forgetteth what manner of man he was.

But whoso looketh into the perfect law of liberty, and *continueth* therein, he being not a forgetful hearer, but a doer of the work, this man shall be blessed in his deed.

If *any man* among you seem to be religious, and bridleth not his tongue, but deceiveth his own heart, this man's religion is vain.

Pure religion and undefiled before God and the Father is this, To visit the fatherless and widows in their affliction, and to keep himself unspotted from the world. (James 1: 22–27)

THE HOLY SPIRIT NEVER EASES His pressure upon us about our salvation with this all-important "if."

Anyone who is a hearer of the Word but not a doer is self-deceived. His "religion is vain." His religion is a false make-believe; it is hypocritical pretention. He moves always in the orbit of his polluted self-interests. Sacrifice and holiness are words for the dictionary. They have no part in the spiritual language of his life. To him, consecration is a word that has lost its meaning. But he talks often about a sovereign will that gives him a once-saved-always-saved hope.

"But be ye doers of the word." The meaning of the Greek text is: "keep on becoming doers of the word." "Keep himself unspotted from the world"—"keep on keeping himself unspotted from the world." Whoso looketh into the Word and *continueth* therein is not deceived. This idea of continuous action in the things of God is one of the most emphasized truths in the Greek New Testament.

One of Isaiah's prophecies that has mass fulfillment today was quoted by Jesus: "This people draweth nigh unto me with their mouth, and honoureth me with their lips; but their heart is far from me" (Matt. 15:8).

Observe the conditions of the texts: Whoever does not continue in God's Word; whoever does not bridle his tongue; whoever does not continually keep himself pure and undefiled before God; whoever does not take his share of the world's sorrow and visit the fatherless and widow; whoever does not keep himself unspotted from the world—he is self-deceived and his religion is in "vain." If he continues in sin instead of continuing to fulfill the conditions of salvation, he is predestinated to be lost.

There are two more ifs in chapter 2:8, 9, but we have passed over many ifs in the progress of our argument. In verses 17–26, we read:

Even so faith, *if* it hath not works, is dead, being alone . . .

But wilt thou know, O vain man, that faith without works is dead?

Was not Abraham our father justified by works, when he had offered Isaac his son upon the altar?

Seest thou how faith wrought with his works, and by works was faith made perfect?

Likewise also was not Rahab the harlot justified by works, when she had received the messengers, and had sent them out another way?

For as the body without the spirit is dead, so faith without works is dead also.

The Apostle told here how faith can be *identified*. Faith, if alone, is powerless to save. But if it has the activating and energizing component of works, it is saving faith.

"If it hath not works." Again the Greek tense is emphatic: "If it keep on not having works"—it is dead. When a man is alive, there is *evidence* that he is alive. When he is dead, there is evidence that he is dead. Works are proofs of living faith. The absence of works is proof of dead faith. Those with saving faith can be *identified*—by their works.

The Apostle challenged all: "Shew me thy faith without thy works, and I will shew thee my faith by my works" (v. 18). Faith cannot *prove* its existence without works. Paul, in Galatians 5:6, told about "faith which worketh [is energized] by love."

James illustrated his faith-works doctrine with Abraham. "*Seest* thou how faith *wrought with* his works." Abraham offered up Isaac by faith and works. Faith alone or works alone would not have made Abraham acceptable to God. Faith in the heart cannot be seen, but faith expressing itself through works is easily seen. If saving faith cannot be seen, it doesn't exist.

Another seest-thou illustration was that of Rahab. She was justified by works when she hid the spies and helped them escape. Rahab's faith was *exhibited* by her works. Suppose Rahab had told the spies: "I have faith; I am a believer in your God, but I cannot betray my country and endanger my life to save yours." Would she have been saved? No, that would have been *dead faith*, and she would have died when Joshua's army marched into Jericho. She would have died with a dead faith.

The eleventh chapter of Hebrews has forty verses. One verse (the first) tells us what faith *is*. The rest of the chapter tells us what faith *does*. Conversely, many talk much about faith in predestinating grace, but neglect the things that genuine faith does. When people do not give a Bible truth the importance that God gives it — BEWARE.

James stressed faith-works and their coordinating dependence—their interacting effect upon each other. The Great Day will reveal that much modern preaching is deceptive because it teaches faith without a proportionate emphasis on works.

James said that as the body is dead without the spirit, so faith without works is dead. Works are to faith what spirit is to the body. A dead man has a body but the body has no spirit. If it did, it would *act*. There would be a seest-thou evidence.

Salvation is of the Jews. This salvation is founded on the conditional Abrahamic Covenant. Abraham is "the father of us all." He faithfully obeyed the conditions of the covenant God gave him. God's predestinating grace does not save without this faith-works principle.

Do you, dear reader, have the faith-works of a soul-saving experience that can be *seen*, or a faith-alone experience that cannot be seen and which cannot save you? Do you, like Abraham, bring to God's altar the faith-works of a costly sacrifice, or the unbelief and cheapness of a Cain-sacrifice?

13

The If-Condition in the

General Epistles

SECOND PETER

Whereby are given unto us exceeding great and precious promises: that by these ye might be partakers of the divine nature, having escaped the corruption that is in the world through lust.

And beside this, giving all diligence, add to your faith virtue; and to virtue knowledge;

And to knowledge temperance; and to temperance patience; and to patience godliness:

And to godliness brotherly kindness; and to brotherly kindness charity.

For *if* these things be in you, and abound, *they make you* that ye shall neither be barren nor unfruitful in the knowledge of our Lord Jesus Christ.

But he that lacketh *these things* is blind, and cannot see afar off, and hath forgotten that he was purged from his old sins.

Wherefore the rather, brethren, give diligence to make your calling and election sure: for *if ye do these things*, ye shall never fall. (II Pet. 1: 4–10)

GOD'S EXCEEDING GREAT and precious promises are given to us that by obedience and faith through them we become partakers of the divine nature. To this purpose we must give all diligence. We must make every effort by the exercise of faith to add to our souls all spiritual goodness, knowledge, self-control, stedfastness, godliness, brotherly kindness, and love.

The development of these spiritual qualities make us that we be neither barren nor unfruitful in the Lord. He that lacks these things is blind and barren in the Lord and hath forgotten that he was "purged from his old sins." Peter speaks of those who had been once saved but had not made their calling and election sure by doing "these things." You may agree that anyone who had been purged from his old sins had been saved.

Peter speaks of those once-saved people over whom the mastery of sin had regained control. They were blind and could not see afar off like the heroes of faith in Hebrews 11: 13. They could not see heavenly things. Their spiritual eyes were diseased. They could not see God's interests, but with eagle-eyed vision they could see to the depths of their own selfish interests. With sharp vision they saw every detail of their money and possessions but stumbled over the things of God in the darkness of their blinded souls. As one must *do* these things to make his salvation sure, then the salvation of those who do them not is unsure. Jesus said some astonishing things about darkness.

> The light of the body is the eye: *if* therefore thine eye be single, thy whole body shall be full of light.

> But *if* thine eye be evil, thy whole body shall be full of darkness. If therefore the light that is in thee be darkness, how great is that darkness! (Matt. 6: 22, 23)

> Take heed therefore that the light which is in thee be not darkness. (Luke 11: 35)

> Walk while ye have the light, lest darkness come
> upon you: for he that walketh in darkness know-
> eth not whither he goeth. (John 12: 35)

> And this is the condemnation, that light is come
> into the world, and men loved darkness rather than
> light, because their deeds were evil. (John 3: 19)

All who love darkness shall in the end be "cast
out into outer darkness" (Matt. 8: 12). All who love
the light make their calling and election sure by doing "these things." They continue to do these things
and the eternal purpose ever deepens and widens
in their souls as they progress toward the end.

Jesus taught in these Scriptures that our only
security against darkness is to continually walk in
the light. Those who do this have a "single eye."
David said: *"One thing* have I desired of the Lord,
that will I seek after; that I may dwell in the house
of the Lord all the days of my life" (Ps. 27: 4). Paul
said: "This *one thing* I do, forgetting those things
which are behind, and reaching [straining] forth
unto those things which are before, I press toward
the mark for the prize" (Phil. 3: 13, 14). "A double
minded man is unstable in all his ways" (James 1: 8).
The athlete in Paul's Olympic illustration knew the
importance of keeping his eye on the goal. Those
who continue in sin continue to pass into a deeper
state of darkness and death. It is a deadly progression that leads to "a sin unto death."

We do not save ourselves. We cannot save ourselves, but by giving heart-cooperation to God's
conditions for salvation, we make it possible for
His mercy and grace to save us.

Peter told Calvinists, Arminians, Eternal Securitists, and all: "Give diligence to make your calling
and election sure: for if ye do these things, ye shall
never fall." Those who do these things are God's
predestinated ones. These are the ones who shall

never perish; nor can anyone pluck them out of God's hand. Neither death, nor life, nor Satan, nor anything can ever separate them from God's love.

Theologians are puzzled about the mysterious relation between the divine and human wills. But what is unrevealed need not trouble us. We are concerned with what *is* revealed, and that is the conditions of salvation. Peter, in his First Epistle (1:2), wrote:

> Elect according to the foreknowledge of God the Father, through sanctification of the Spirit, unto obedience and sprinkling of the blood of Jesus Christ.

Here again is evidence that in the Scriptures election or predestination does not stand alone as unconditional but has conditional connectives. It is through sanctification of the Spirit—unto obedience. This is what we have argued all the way from Genesis. Did you ever hear an Eternal Security teacher make election conditional upon sanctification and obedience?

Peter said God's calling and election is sure for those who "make" it so. Jesus is the Surety of God's salvation covenant (Heb. 7:22). The Divine Elector chose sanctification, obedience, and Calvary's covenant blood as means to make salvation sure. His *Covenant of Surety* is certain for all who remain under the security of the "sprinkling of the blood of Jesus Christ."

Salvation is of the Jews. Peter, a Jew, made salvation conditional upon the successive performance of acts specified in the covenant. Peter asked:

> And *if* the righteous scarcely be saved, where shall the ungodly and the sinner appear? (I Pet. 4:18)

If the righteous, because of the sharp trials, sufferings, and testings, are saved with difficulty, where shall those appear who continue in sin? What is *your* answer to Peter's question?

14

The If-Condition in the
General Epistles

FIRST JOHN

If we say that we have fellowship with him, and
walk in darkness, we lie, and do not the truth;

But *if* we walk in the light, as he is in the light,
we have fellowship one with another, and the blood
of Jesus Christ his Son cleanseth us from all sin.
(I John 1: 6, 7)

"IF WE WALK IN THE LIGHT. . . ." Greek: "If we
keep on walking in the light we have partnership
one with another, and the blood of Jesus Christ
cleanseth us from all sin." There is no cleansing
from sin, and no salvation, without a continual walking in God's light. One part of the sentence is co-
ordinate with the other. We must walk always in
the light, and we must "walk *even as* he walked"
(I John 2: 6).

But whoso keepeth his word, in him verily is the
love of God perfected: hereby know we that we
are in him. (I John 2: 5)

Whoso keepeth on keeping on in God's Word is
in God. Hereby know we that we are in God. The
continuity test reveals who is of God and who is

not. In times of religious excitement and emotional stirrings, some may *appear* to be saved but the test proves who is genuine and who is counterfeit.

> And *hereby* we do know that we know him, *if* we keep his commandments. (I John 2:3)

> If ye know that he is righteous, ye know that every one that doeth righteousness [continually] is born of him. (I John 2:29)

In chapter 2:19, the Apostle told how the hypocrites and counterfeiters were revealed in his time:

> They went out from us, but they were not of us; for *if* they had been of us, they would no doubt have *continued* with us: but they went out, that they might be made manifest that they were not all of us.

The persons described here were in the Christian church. They *seemed* to be religious. They had the appearance of true Christians—until they were tried by a test that revealed their true characters—and that was the continuity test. In this character-revealing test, they withdrew from the truth; they withdrew from the saints and went out to join forces with the antichrist spirit already in the world. Those who continue not in righteousness are against Christ. "He that is not with me is against me" (Luke 11:23). John said they were "made manifest" by the test. And in the sight of God and man, everyone will be *made manifest.*

> Let that therefore abide in you, which ye have heard from the beginning. *If* that which ye have heard from the beginning shall *remain* in you, ye also shall continue in the Son, and in the Father. (I John 2:24)

Observe the force of this if-continue text. John told his hearers they would continue in the Father and Son *if* what they had heard from the beginning remained (continually) in them. In 4:12 he said:

If we love one another, God dwelleth in us. . . .

Those who enter the Kingdom of God must first pass the qualifying tests. These tests have exposed the false profession of many. "He that doeth the will of God [continually] abideth for ever" (2:17). They abide forever because "the word of God abideth" (continually) in them (2:14).

> Little children, let no man deceive you: he that doeth righteousness is righteous, even as he is righteous. *He that committeth sin is of the devil.* (I John 3:7, 8).

Salvation is of the Jews. The Apostle John, a Jew, put much emphasis on the if-condition. With repeated stress he said that by this test it could be determined who is of God and who is not. He who continues in righteousness is of God. He who continues in sin is of the devil.

15

Salvation Conditional in the Epistle of Jude

THE APOSTLE JUDE used three warnings to teach that salvation is conditional. He showed that in the eternal universe of God's moral creatures, obedience to His moral laws is a condition of acceptance with Him. This truth extends to all time and space. It includes the human and angelic order of moral beings. Jude presented three cases from the history of Israel, angels, and Sodom and Gomorrha.

I will therefore put you in remembrance, though ye once knew this, how that the Lord, having *saved* the people out of the land of Egypt, afterward destroyed them that believed not.

And the angels which kept not their first estate, but left their own habitation, he hath reserved in everlasting chains under darkness unto the judgment of the great day.

Even as Sodom and Gomorrha, and the cities about them in like manner, giving themselves over to fornication, and going after strange flesh, are set forth for an example, suffering the vengeance of eternal fire. (Jude 5–7)

. . .God spared not the angels that sinned, but cast them down to hell, and delivered them into chains of darkness, to be reserved unto judgment. (II Pet. 2:4)

Jude first used the oft-repeated "example" of Israel. God, with miracles of deliverance, "saved" Israel from Egyptian slavery. This word *save-saved* is used 94 times in the New Testament. It is the same word used when Jesus "saved" sinners. To a sinner, Jesus said: "Thy faith hath saved thee; go in peace" (Luke 7:50). "For the Son of man is come to seek and to save that which was lost" (Luke 19:10). "Whosoever shall call on the name of the Lord shall be saved" (Acts 2:21). "If thou shalt confess with thy mouth the Lord Jesus...thou shalt be saved" (Rom. 10:9). These and many other references show the New Testament meaning of saved.

Not only was Israel miraculously saved from Egypt but they were sustained by a miraculous salvation in the desert for 40 years. God said Israel "saw my works forty years" (Heb. 3:9). They all ate "the same spiritual meat; and they did all drink the same spiritual drink: for they drank of that spiritual Rock that followed them: and that Rock was Christ" (I Cor. 10:4). They saw and experienced a miraculous salvation for 40 years — and died in unbelief. They fell from their high position of covenant privilege, never to enter the Promised Land; and God swore they would never enter "My rest." Lost forever!

Paul and Jude said the Israelites were our examples, and their saved-lost history was written for our admonition. There is a contrast in Jude's text: "The Lord *having saved* the people...*afterward destroyed* them that believed not." This is the opposite of "once saved, always saved." Jude taught: Once saved, afterward destroyed. The once-saved always-saved teaching denies the facts of Biblical language.

Jude's second illustration was about the angels. They violated the moral conditions under which God placed them. They "kept not their first estate, but *left* their own habitation." This indicates their existence in the "first estate" was subject to conditions. With their own power of decision they left this habitation. They did not *continue* in it, and are reserved in everlasting chains unto the judgment of the great day. There is no redemption for them. "God *spared* not the angels that *sinned*." And, "God *spared* not the natural branches; take heed lest he also *spare* not thee" (Rom. 11:21).

The angels could—and did—forfeit their state of eternal life. And some claim that eternal life is "unforfeitable!" Sin is sin, and sinners are sinners, whether they be human sinners or angelic sinners.

If angels had obeyed the conditions and *continued* in their estate, they would still be in that state of eternal life instead of in everlasting chains. All violators of God's holy laws, whether Israelites, angels, or Sodomites, will be punished with the same "vengeance of eternal fire." Concerning the sin of the angels, the *Expositors Greek Testament* [1] says:

> This of course supplies an even more striking instance of the possibility of falling from grace.

Perhaps no Bible commentary holds a position of higher esteem than does the *Pulpit Commentary,* and in its exposition of these judgments on Israel and angels, says:

> The second instance of Divine judgment is taken from the angelic world. The copula (*and*) connects it closely with the former and gives it some emphasis, "angels too," i,e, angels not less than people selected by God to be a people for himself have been examples of the terrible Divine retribution.

These Israelic sinners, angelic sinners, and Sodomic sinners are all classed together in the above

---

[1] V. 5, p. 259.

Scriptures. These and all who have likewise sinned will go to the same place of eternal punishment. Jesus, in the judgment, will say to all sinners before Him:

> Depart from me, ye cursed, into everlasting fire, prepared for the devil and his angels. (Matt. 25: 41)

Jude said the three judgments are "set forth for an example." This word "example" (Gr. *deigma*) means: "primarily a thing shown, a specimen ... denotes an example given as a warning." [2] "Something, therefore, which is held up to view as a warning." [3]

Jude's warning examples were for those who were "turning the grace of God into lasciviousness," and who disowned the Lord (v. 4). These perverters were abusing God's grace and committing lawless acts of lust and immorality. Like the Jewish examples, they continued in these sins.

How can those, who profess salvation, be finally saved when they continue in the same sins of the Jewish examples? And there are large numbers today who make such a profession who habitually live in the same sins that excluded the Jews from the Promised Land and God's rest.

Salvation is of the Jews. Jude reminded us that multitudes of Jews and angels, who were once saved, are now bound in eternal chains.

It is a dangerous deception for anyone to think that Jude's saved-lost Jewish warning does not apply to him. He should remember that even with the angels there was no such security as "once in heaven, always in heaven."

---

[2] *Vine's Dictionary of New Testament Words*, V. 2, p. 54.
[3] *Vincent's Word Studies*, V. I, p. 714.

16

The If-Condition in Revelation

> Remember therefore how thou hast received and heard, and hold fast, and repent. *If* therefore thou shalt not watch, I will come on thee as a thief, and thou shalt not know what hour I will come upon thee.
>
> Thou hast a few names even in Sardis which have not defiled their garments; and *they* shall walk with me in white: for they are worthy.
>
> He that overcometh, *the same* shall be clothed in white raiment; and I will not blot out his name out of the book of life, but I will confess his name before my Father, and before his angels. (Rev. 3:3–5)

IN THE ACTS WE READ of multitudes who were attracted to the gospel in the cities of Europe and Asia. Large churches were established by the Apostles. But before the century ended, serious changes had developed in these churches. The Lord had made various attempts to correct this decayed spiritual condition but His warnings were unheeded. Finally He sent an ultimatum. Repentance was the only hope held out to them.

In chapter 2:1–7, Christ told the Ephesian church: "Thou hast left thy first love." And He threatened: "I will come unto thee quickly, and will remove thy candlestick out of his place, except thou repent." Their removal was conditional upon their repentance. He also told this church:

> To him that overcometh will I give to eat of the tree of life, which is in the midst of the paradise of God.

To eat of the tree of life was conditional. One must be an overcomer to eat of the tree of life. What they had to overcome was the loss of their first love. This loss of love to God and neighbor is widespread in Christianity today, and it has been our observation that few ever regain it. Christ taught here that regaining lost love is a condition for eating of the tree of life.

To the church in Smyrna, Christ wrote (Rev. 2: 10, 11):

> Fear none of those things which thou shalt suffer: behold, the devil shall cast some of you into prison, that ye may be *tried;* . . . be thou faithful unto death, and I will give thee a crown of life.

> He that overcometh shall not be hurt of the second death.

Christ promised the crown of life to those who continued faithful in their testings and provings. He required that they be faithful in their trials and that they remain faithful unto death. "Keep on becoming faithful . . . keep on proving faithful unto death" (Robertson). They were *proved* that they might be *approved* for the crown of life. Those faithful unto death would not be hurt of the second death.

The crown-of-life promise was to the overcomer. The word "overcome" appears 28 times in the New Testament. Of these, 17 are here in Revelation. God allowed various testings to prove the churches. In each of these seven churches there was a particular thing to be overcome. The promises were only for overcomers who endured unto the end. This agrees with other texts we have seen. "He that endureth unto the end, the same shall be saved." "Blessed is the man that endureth temptation: for *when* he is *tried,* he shall receive the crown of life."

> If a Christian keep himself loyal till death, the prophet here guarantees that Christ will keep him safe after death.[1]

The church at Thyatira had become infected with a deadly evil. Christ sent an ultimatum of spiritual death to them (Rev. 2:20–23).

> Notwithstanding I have a few things against thee, because thou sufferest that woman Jezebel, which calleth herself a prophetess, to teach and to seduce my servants to commit fornication. . . .
>
> I gave her space to repent . . . and she repented not.
>
> And I will kill her children with death; and all the churches shall know that I am he which searcheth the reins and hearts.

Jezebel was the symbolic name for the historic and wicked Jezebel, one of the most evil influences in Israelic history. She killed the true prophets of God (I Kings 18:13), but gathered round her 400 false prophets. These she attached to her sanctuary at Jezreel and fed them at her table. She was the high priestess of a corrupt religion. She had been long dead but her teaching and spirit survived and had infiltrated the Thyatira church. (When an Old Testament character appears in the New Testament, take note and study it carefully, and you will learn something valuable.)

We have seen before that God's covenant with Israel was a covenant of matrimony—Jehovah-Husband and Israel-Wife. Paul told the Corinthians he

---

[1] *Expositors Greek Testament,* V. 5, p. 355.

was jealous for them because he had betrothed them to one husband that he might present them as a "chaste virgin to Christ" (II Cor. 11:2). But Paul was afraid they were corrupted by the harlot spirit, for there was much of it in Corinth.

The old spirit of lustful harlotry that caused Israel to be struck down in the wilderness had reappeared in Thyatira, and Christ sent them the death-threat. Under Mosaic marriage law, a Jewess was put to death if she was unfaithful to her *covenant of betrothal*. Christ likewise threatened the spiritual harlots in Thyatira with spiritual death. The union would then be dissolved. "I will kill her children with death." It was a "sin unto death" (I John 5:16).

At the beginning of this chapter we quoted the if-threat Christ sent to Sardis. Christ would come upon them as a thief *if* they did not watch for His coming. In God's order of things, there comes the time when all who are neglectful get their last chance. The threatened judgment for Sardis could be avoided by their obedience to the if-condition.

There were a few names in Sardis who had not defiled their garments. In Scripture, the wearing of garments represents the spiritual life. The faithful few in Sardis had kept themselves from the lust-stains that had defiled the garments of others. The promise to walk with Christ in white was only to overcomers, for "they are worthy."

> The merit is not theirs, but Christ's, in whose blood they have washed their robes...and by whose grace they are preserved in holiness. It is because they have by God's help fulfilled the conditions which he has promised to accept, that they are worthy.[2]

---

[2] *Pulpit Commentary.*

To those who were overcomers (continually) in Sardis, Christ promised that He would not blot their names out of the book of life. This blotting out of a name from the book of life has caused much controversy. Some argue: "Can a name be blotted out of the book of life, once it is written in it?" Christ would not threaten them with an impossibility. The difficulty vanishes when these words are considered in the light of the historical idea that Christ referred to.

> For a name to be erased from the book of life (one's deeds not corresponding, upon scrutiny, to one's position: cf. 20:12, Jub. 36:10) meant condemnation, or exclusion from the heavenly kingdom. . . .

> For the erasure of names from the civic register, consequent upon their owner's condemnation, cf. Dio Chrys. xxxi, 336.[3]

> A register of citizens was kept in ancient states: the names of the dead were erased.[4]

> Here we seem to have a figure borrowed from the custom of striking the names of the dead out of the list of citizens.[5]

When an Israelite violated Mosaic covenant law, God said: "Whosoever hath sinned against me, him will I blot out of my book" (Ex. 32:33; Deut. 29:20). The sinning Israelite was "cut off" from God's covenant register by death (Ps. 69:28). Genealogy records were kept for members of the covenant Commonwealth. Records like those listed in Matthew 1 and Luke 3 had great importance for Jews. In ancient Athens and Rome, citizens were put to death for crimes against the state and their names re-

---

[3] *Expositors Greek Testament*, V. 5, p. 365.

[4] *Jamieson, Fausset, Brown Commentary.*

[5] *Pulpit Commentary.*

moved from the civic register. No nation had un-conditional citizenship.

The names of God's elect shall never be removed from the book of life. They remain faithful. They continually keep the if-conditions. The angels do not rejoice over names blotted from the book; their re-joicing is for the names that shall never be removed.

The sins and negligence of the Sardis people had made them careless about the Lord's coming. The re-lation of Christ's coming to the spiritual condition of this church has much meaning. Many churches today have little or no interest in our Lord's return. And when He comes and finds them in defiled gar-ments, not watching and not overcoming, He will enforce His threats against them. Christ made ev-erything depend upon obedience to the if-conditions. There is proof for this in Christ's ultimatum to Sar-dis.

The Bible ends with magnificent wedding scenes. An author unfolds his plot at the end of his book. In Revelation, chapters 19–22, there are many glori-ous details about the Bridegroom, Bride, Bridal Supper, and Bridal City. The announcement of this wedding brought mighty hosannas from heaven's multitudes that sounded like a thunderstorm.

> And I heard as it were the voice of a great mul-titude, and as the voice of many waters, and as the voice of mighty thunderings, saying, Alleluia: for the Lord God omnipotent reigneth.
>
> Let us be glad and rejoice, and give honour to him: for the marriage of the Lamb is come, and his wife hath made herself ready.
>
> And to her was granted that she should be arrayed in fine linen, clean and white: for the fine linen is the righteousness of saints. (Rev. 19:6–8)

This is the event for which God, angels, and men have waited. It is the final unveiling of the "mystery" frequently referred to in Scripture. This is the destination of predestination. This predestinated Bride enters into marriage with her glorious Bridegroom and forever enjoys her wedlock with Him.

The thunderous announcement specified that "his wife hath made herself ready"; and it directed attention to the Bride's dress. It was "granted" to her to be arrayed in the bridal dress for which she had "made herself ready." Both Bridegroom and Bride had cooperated in preparation for her wedding attire. The wedding robe was of fine linen, clean and white; for the fine linen is "the righteousness of saints," or, "the righteous acts of saints." Isaiah (61:10) wrote about "garments of salvation," and "robe of righteousness." In ancient times, harlots were punished by shaving their heads (I Cor. 11:5) and dressing them in black.

The Bride had made herself ready for the wedding by the past action of her righteous life. She had continually kept her salvation garments and had been faithful to her nuptial vows. This preparation would have been impossible if she had continued in sin instead of continuing in the marriage covenant. Her part in the wedding was conditional upon making herself ready for it.

Christ's faithful Bride stands in contrast to the Harlot of Revelation 17:1–5. The Bride represents the body of faithful believers who continue in righteousness; the Harlot represents the body of the unfaithful who continue in sin. She is not only a harlot, but the "mother of harlots." Her "golden cup" of apostate religion is "filled with the filthiness of her fornication." Goddess of religion, and empress of the earth, she is a filthy and drunken fornicatress whom the world adores and worships.

Today, Babylon the Great spreads its deadly system of unholy religion over the world in preparation for the coming of Antichrist. It has none of Christ's conditions for salvation. If it did, it could not deceive the nations. You can join it and continue in sin, for it has no condition except compliance with its fatal delusion. It is Easy-Religion, Inc.

Let us now listen to "him that speaketh from heaven" (Heb. 12:25), as He neared the end of His message to the churches in Revelation.

> Blessed are they that do his commandments, that they may have right to the tree of life, and may enter in through the gates into the city. (Rev. 22: 14)

Some translations have this verse: "Blessed are those who cleanse their garments that they may have right to the tree of life." Those who cleanse their garments are those who keep His commandments. Take it either way, the right to the tree of life is *conditional*. To deny this, one must deny the reality of facts.

Salvation is of the Jews. And four times here in Revelation the Lion of Judah and Root of David (5:5; 22:16) made eternal life conditional. In 2:7, the promise to eat of the tree of life was given to him who continually overcomes. In 2:10, the crown of life was promised to those who, being tested, were faithful unto death. In 2:11, the continual overcomer would not be hurt of the second death. In 22:14, the right to the tree of life is promised to those who continually cleanse their garments and keep His commandments.

Here are our last ifs:

> *If* any man thirst, let him come unto me and drink. (John 7:37)

> And the Spirit and the bride say, Come. And let him that heareth say, Come. And let him that is athirst come. And whosoever will, let him take the water of life freely. (Rev. 22:17)

> Behold, I stand at the door, and knock: *if* any
> man hear my voice, and open the door, I will come
> in to him, and will sup with him, and he with me.
> (Rev. 3:20)

These promises are for "any man" who thirsts. This is the condition. No sinner or backslider need despair if he desires to find God. Eternal life is within his reach if he will repent and believe. None need fear predestination if he will come to God with a hungry soul. God's love and mercy are exceeding great. Some in deepest depravity, like Saul of Tarsus, found mercy. "Smoking flax shall he not quench" (Matt. 12:20). In the darkness there may be yet a ray of hope. Let anyone who is troubled about predestination come to God thirsting; let him forsake sin and come to God's altar with all that he has, and all that he is, and God will enter into a covenant of eternal life with him.

17

Summary of Evidence

1. We submitted historical facts about the doctrine of predestination as taught by the 5th century church father, Augustine, who, so far as is known, was the first to teach the doctrine of unconditional salvation.

2. We quoted Professor Seeberg, a doctrinal historian friendly to Augustine, who said there was "a multitude of inconsistencies and self-contradictory tendencies in his teaching." Even Augustine's Benedictine editors admitted he was badly equipped for the work of interpretation. Augustine laid down rules of interpretation for his opponents on other doctrines, but he consistently violated his own rules in his interpretation of the predestination Scriptures.

Other historians agree with Professor Seeberg's opinion of Augustine's self-contradictory tendencies in his teachings.

Dr. K. R. Hagenbach in his *A History of Christian Doctrines*[1] wrote:

> But the doctrine in question [Augustine's predestination] became to many a stone of stumbling which orthodox theologians them-

---

[1] V. 1, pp. 429–430. London, 1880.

selves, specially those of the Greek Church, endeavored by every possible means to remove.

The noted professor of church history, Adolph Harnack, of Berlin (1851–1930), in his famous work, *History of Dogma*,[2] wrote:

> "Augustine contradicted himself . . ." (p. 217). His doctrinal teachings were "a bundle of inconsistencies and extremely questionable ideas" (p. 209). His doctrinal teaching was "an impious and foolish dogma" (p. 217). "Augustine's contradictions were enormous" (p. 220). His teaching was "beset by inconsistency" (p. 220).

3. Historical information was given about John Calvin who taught Augustine's unconditional salvation. Augustine was Calvin's guiding light. We quoted two leading doctrinal historians friendly to Calvin, Professor Seeberg and Dean Farrar:

> Calvin found the . . . fatal facility of reading into Scripture what he wished to find there. [Calvin] had a manner in which he explains away every passage which runs counter to his dogmatic prepossessions. [His interpretations had] "many defects."

Calvin never proved his unconditional salvation, so he gave us the feeble plea that it is a mystery hidden in the "secret counsel of God," and that it is a subject of "considerable difficulty," "very perplexed," and those who "pry" into it will find themselves in an "inextricable labyrinth."[3]

Calvin, like Augustine, laid down fair rules of interpretation for his opponents on other doc-

---

[2] V. 5, Williams & Nargate, London, 1898.
[3] Institute, Book 3, Chap. XXI.

trines but he consistently violated his own rules in his interpretations of the predestination Scriptures. It is a fair requirement that an interpreter be consistent with himself. Augustine and Calvin were not.

4. Our premise was based on Jesus' statement: "Salvation is of the Jews." As salvation was founded on conditional Jewish covenants, it is therefore conditional upon obedience to these covenant laws.

5. Salvation was conditional from the beginning. God told Cain: "If thou doest well, shalt thou not be accepted?" Cain did not obey this condition and was rejected. His religious "works were evil." The New Testament warns us about the "way of Cain." It is a way of deception because it rejects God's condition for salvation. Cain refused God's if-condition and "went out from the presence of the Lord" (Gen. 4: 16).

6. The New Testament covenant of salvation is founded on God's covenant with Abraham. The Kingdom of God is also founded on the Abrahamic Covenant. Our Saviour was slain from the foundation of the world, but He was the "seed of Abraham." Although salvation was promised before the foundation of the world, it was channeled through the Abrahamic Covenant.

7. It was pointed out that there were four conditions to the Abrahamic Covenant. Abraham obeyed these conditions. Those in his family who broke the covenant would be cut off from the covenant. There was no such security as once in the Covenant, always in the Covenant.

Three times God promised to fulfill His covenant with Abraham: "Because thou hast done this thing"—"Because thou hast obeyed my voice"—"Because that Abraham obeyed my voice, and kept my charge, my commandments, my statutes, and my laws."

8. Salvation is of the Jews. The Sinai Covenant was made with the Jews. This was a further development of the Abrahamic Covenant and it contained many if-conditions. It was ratified with the Jews only after they had given their consent to its conditions. Many references were given to show that the death penalty was inflicted upon covenant violators. Moses often warned them of the covenant "if" and threatened them with the covenant curses for breach of covenant. Three thousand years of dreadful Jewish history bear shocking witness to the fact that these curses fell upon them. *The Amplified Old Testament*[4] takes the position that the Sinai Covenant was conditional and that its fulfillment depended upon Israel's continual faithfulness to the covenant. The evidence is strong and conclusive for the fact that the Sinai Covenant was an if-covenant.

9. The Abrahamic and Sinaitic Covenants were carried through and further developed in the Davidic Covenant. We cited many references to prove that this covenant was conditional. God, David, and Solomon repeated and emphasized the "if" in their covenant negotiations. Under this Davidic Covenant, Israelites were executed for disobedience to its laws. The evidence fully supports the fact that the Davidic Covenant was an if-covenant.

Dr. Patrick Fairbairn (1805–74) is widely quoted as an authority on Biblical interpretation, and concerning the fulfillment of the Davidic Covenant, he wrote:

---

4 Part One, p. 701, Zondervan

> ...David himself knew perfectly, that there
> was an implied condition, which might render
> such a thing possible, and that the prophecy
> behoved to be read in the light of those great
> principles which pervade the whole of the
> Divine economy.[5]

10. In the Prophets, we saw unified emphasis on the if-condition. The breach of covenant threats were constantly held before the Jews by the prophets. The covenant "if" was repeated by Samuel, Azariah, Isaiah, Hezekiah, Nehemiah, Jeremiah, Ezekiel, Zechariah, and Malachi.

11. We cited 63 if-texts in the Old Testament to prove the Jewish covenants conditional. From God's "if" to Cain, to Malachi's "if" to the priests, the unified testimony of Scripture gives full approval to our doctrine of conditional salvation.

12. The New Covenant is the fulfillment of the Abrahamic-Davidic Covenants. Jesus was the "son of David, the son of Abraham" (Matt. 1:1). The old covenants moved toward Christ for their fulfillment. We proved these covenants conditional. As we reason from one covenant to another, it follows that the New Covenant is also conditional.

13. The Old and New Covenants were not indifferent to the requirements of moral law. Christ included the if-condition in His moral laws in the Sermon on the Mount.

14. Other if-proofs were cited from Jesus' teachings. No man could be His disciple unless he forsook all and followed Him. Only those who passed His if-tests were genuine disciples. "If ye continue in my word, then are ye my disciples indeed." "If any man will come after me, let him

---

[5] *The Interpretation of Prophecy*, p. 66, London, 1964.

deny himself, and take up his cross, and follow
me." "If a man keep my sayings, he shall never
see death" (John 8:51). Christ's if-conditions
for salvation were severe.

15. Christ exposed the hypocrisy of the Jews with
the Abrahamic works-test. These Jews boasted
of their security in the Abrahamic Covenant.
Christ replied: "If ye were Abraham's children,
ye would do the *works* of Abraham."

Christ required the same evidence of faith
for salvation in the New Covenant that God required in the Abrahamic Covenant. The Abrahamic Covenant is embodied in the New Covenant; therefore, salvation is conditional in the
New as in the Abrahamic.

16. Christ further warned the Jews about their false
security. The Jews of Capernaum and other cities of Israel would be "thrust down to hell."
The men of Nineveh would rise in the judgment
and condemn them because they repented at
the preaching of Jonah but the Jews did not repent at the preaching of Jesus (Matt. 11:20–24;
12:41, 42). Repentance and a turning to righteousness were conditions to avert condemnation
at the judgment.

17. The if-emphasis Jesus gave to the New Covenant was continued by the apostles. Paul used
the covenant "if" in his predestination teaching
to the Romans. He said the Jews were "broken
off" their covenant tree "because of unbelief,"
and that they would be grafted in again only
"if they abide not still in unbelief."

18. Paul taught that salvation was an if-covenant for
both Jews and Gentiles. The Gentiles were grafted to Israel's covenant tree because of their faith;
but Paul held the if-warning before them. They
would remain in Israel's covenant tree of salva-

tion "if thou continue in his goodness, otherwise thou also shalt be cut off." Those who did not continue in covenant obedience, both Jews and Gentiles, would be cut off. Jesus taught the same about those who did not abide in the Vine (John 15:6).

19. Top lexical authorities were quoted for the Biblical definitions of predestination, election, and foreknowledge. In these definitions there was not even a hint of unconditional salvation. This Foreknowledge knew what men would do with their free choice, but freedom of decision is at the controls of human actions.

   Jesus "knew *what was in man.*" This text teaches that the *cause* of man's moral action is *what is in man,* and not in a mysterious predestination. The laws of cause are the laws of reason.

   God endowed man with the ability to choose his own way. Divine influences are exerted to persuade him to choose God's way, but he is free to decide. His eternal destiny is an act of his own determination. His eternal choice is decided by his own will.

   All things come into existence according to God's creative purposes, but man has freedom of decision concerning his salvation. This fact is stated or assumed throughout the Bible.

   The apostles, like Jesus, constantly argued from the moral character of the older covenants and applied their moral teachings in the New Testament. Moral law is interwoven throughout the covenant system, and unconditional salvation would be intolerable to moral justice.

20. In the expression, "Jacob have I loved, but Esau have I hated," we quoted Greek authorities that "hate" here does not imply malice, but that the

word was used of "relative preference for one thing over another." We showed various facts from the lives of Jacob and Esau as reasons for this relative preference. Those thus selected are elected. Jacob sought the things of God; Esau did not.

21. By the comparative rule of interpretation, we showed the true meaning of: "So then it is not of him that willeth, nor of him that runneth, but of God that sheweth mercy." We proved that other Scriptures require willing and running as conditions of salvation. We used the same rule on the Potter-Clay texts. Eternal Securitists use this rule on other doctrines so it is fair that it be used on predestination.

> The careful comparison of one Scripture with another will generally explain a seeming contradiction.[6]

22. God shows no partiality in salvation. God is love. Both divine and human love is impartial. God cannot be partial because He forbids partiality in us (I Tim. 5:21). "By what He requires of me, I know what God Himself must be" (Whittier). Paul said God was a righteous judge who would give the eternal crown to those who qualify for it (I Tim. 4:7, 8). A righteous judge is impartial.

God showed no unfairness to Pharaoh who hardened his own heart. The heathen Philistines understood that Pharaoh had hardened his own heart and that this was the cause of the severity of God's judgments upon him. They argued that they should not be as Pharaoh, and they sent the ark back to Israel to escape further judgment (I Sam. 6:6).

---

[6] *The Structural Principles of the Bible*, Marsh, F. E., p. 238. Kregel.

23. Lexical proofs from foremost Greek authorities were quoted for the meaning of "castaway." This evidence proved that Paul referred to the possibility of his being disqualified for salvation, not disqualified for Christian service. Paul's illustration about faithless Israel proved what he meant by "castaway." The apostate Israelites under Moses were *castaways,* and Paul said they are our "ensamples," and that their history was written for "our admonition." God said these castaways would never enter His "rest." They are lost forever.

We quoted *Calvin's Commentaries* to show that Calvin interpreted the castaway texts as we do.

24. In Hebrews, we showed that the apostle repeatedly used the if-warning. There was eternal danger in continuing to disobey the conditions of salvation. It is impossible to renew those who "fall away." The apostle warned his readers about what happened to the Jewish examples who *continued in sin.* There was no unconditional security in the Jewish covenants for these Jewish examples.

25. Also, we saw in Hebrews that God said: "They continued not in my covenant, and I regarded them not." In legal language today, such a covenant is called a *Continuing Covenant.* Jesus affirmed the New Testament to be such a covenant with His statement: "If ye continue in my word, then are ye my disciples indeed."

The covenant the Jews did not continue in was the Sinai Covenant, referred to by the prophets as a covenant of wedlock—Jehovah-Husband and Israel-Wife. The "jealous" Husband delivered His harlot wife to her enemies for slavery and death. Christ, weeping over Jerusalem, announced the doom of the Harlot City. The sword of God's vengeance has slashed the Harlot for 19 centuries.

26. We saw other if-texts in Hebrews. "If we sin wilfully after we have received the knowledge of the truth, there remaineth no more sacrifice for sins." He that despised Moses' law died without mercy. Those who despise Christ's covenant will receive "sorer punishment" because it is a greater covenant. This fact proves that salvation in the New Testament is conditional.

27. The warnings in Hebrews were not only for those tempted to deny Christ. The Esau-warning and the root-of-bitterness warning confirm this. Also, "if" they endured chastening, they were God's sons. If not, they were bastards.

28. James said that if any be a hearer of the Word and not a doer, he is self-deceived. Whoever hears the Word and "continueth" therein is not deceived. If any man seems to be religious and does not *keep* (continue) himself pure and undefiled from the world, his "religion is vain." He can be a believer in Eternal Security but he has "believed in vain" (I Cor. 15:2). Multitudes will finally see in the Judgment that their unconditional predestination is "in vain," because they did not obey the conditions that James specified.

29. In James we also saw that faith without works is dead. Faith alone cannot save—and works alone cannot save. We thus avoided two extremes of error. The Bible teaches that Abraham was justified by both faith and works. Paul in Romans stressed Abraham's faith but James stressed his works. The two parts make a whole. Saving faith can be identified by works of faith. Saving faith will do the works of Abraham. Rahab was also justified and saved by faith and

works. She could not have been saved if she had not endangered her life to save Joshua's spies. The Bible tells us much more about what faith does than what faith is.

30. Peter told us to make our calling and election sure. We can make it sure, Peter said, by adding to our salvation God's virtue, knowledge, temperance, and godliness. "If ye *do* these things, ye shall never fall." It follows that the salvation of those who neglect these things is unsure. There is nothing uncertain about God's plan of salvation. It is sure for all who make it sure.

31. Peter also said the saved are "elect according to the foreknowledge of God the Father, through sanctification of the Spirit, unto obedience and sprinkling of the blood of Jesus Christ." Predestination in Scripture does not stand alone. It is related to sanctification and obedience and Jesus' covenant blood. Those who continue in sin do not have this sanctification and covenant blood upon their souls. Their souls have no covenant protection.

Paul taught the same as Peter. "God hath from the beginning chosen you to salvation through sanctification of the Spirit and belief of the truth" (II Thess. 2:13). Paul said here that "from the beginning," that is, from eternity, God had chosen them to salvation *through* sanctification and belief of the truth. The final salvation will be accomplished by means of sanctification and truth. The *Pulpit Commentary* agrees with other leading critical commentaries in its exposition of this verse:

> *Chose you to salvation*—the final purpose of God's election. *Through;* or rather, *in,* denoting the elements in which the salvation consisted or, which is the same thing; the state

into which they were chosen. *Sanctification of the Spirit*—the Divine side—the belief of the truth—the human side of the element in which the salvation was realized.

The *Expositors Greek Testament* agrees with this: ". . . your sanctification and belief in what is true . . . these forming the sphere and scope . . . for salvation being realized. Those who are sanctified and who truly believe shall be saved." "The Divine purpose does not work automatically, but implies the cooperation of Christians . . . a resolute steadfastness resting on loyalty to the apostolic gospel."

When God, from eternity, chose the elect unto salvation, He also chose sanctification and obedience as the means and conditions of their salvation. Predestination in Scripture does not stand alone but has conditional connections. It is unfair and deceptive interpretation that detaches predestination from these connections of sanctification and obedience of truth. It is by the same method of interpretation that other false doctrines are taught by other teachers.

32. John gave us various if-tests by which we could distinguish the true believers from the false— the genuine from the counterfeit. If we walk in the light, Christ's blood cleanses us from sin. We are of God *if* we continually keep His commandments. John applied the *continuity test* to all who claimed salvation.

John said there were some in his day who proved false when put to the continue-test. "If they had been of us, they no doubt would have continued with us." If the truth we have heard "remain" in us, we shall be saved. "He that committeth sin is of the devil." If he continues in sin, he is predestinated to be lost.

> We may assure ourselves of belonging to the number of the elect in so far as we have evidence of our election in our sanctification.[7]

We have seen that God's salvation covenant is a *Continuing Covenant*. And it is a monstrous deception to teach that the continual sinner will be saved by a continuing covenant that demands his continual obedience.

Paul said habitual sinners "treasure up" for themselves "wrath against the day of wrath and revelation of the righteous judgment of God; who will render to every man according to his deeds" (Rom. 2:5, 6). All men will be judged "according to their works" (Rev. 20:13). Their "end shall be according to their works" (II Cor. 11:15).

33. Jude used the oft-repeated warning about the Jewish "examples." The Lord "destroyed" those He had "saved" because they did not continue to believe. Jude also warned his readers about the angels who "kept not their first estate." They are "reserved in everlasting chains" because they "left their own habitation." Even in heaven, there were conditions for remaining there. There was no such security as once in heaven, always in heaven.

34. In Revelation, Jesus threatened the Sardis church with His if-condition. If they did not watch, He would come upon them as a thief. They were required to obey the if-condition to qualify for salvation which was promised to him "that overcometh," meaning, according to the Greek tense, "to him that continues to overcome." Only a "few" in Sardis had continued faithful, and Jesus promised: "*they* shall walk with me in

---

[7] *Pulpit Commentary.*

white: for *they* are worthy." By a law of opposite, non-overcomers shall not walk with Him.

35. Christ allowed various tests to prove the Revelation churches; and again, He connected continual
faithfulness to eternal life: "Be thou faithful
unto death, and I will give thee a crown of life."
The continuity test required: "Keep on becoming
faithful—keep on proving faithful unto death."
Christ said it twice more: "To him that overcometh [continually] will I give to eat of the tree
of life"—"He that overcometh [continually]
shall not be hurt of the second death" (Rev.
2:7–11). Three times here, in verses close together, Christ connected continual victory over
sin with eternal life.

36. Among His ultimatum threats to the churches,
Christ sent a spiritual death threat to the spiritual harlots in Thyatira. "And I will kill her children with death." Repentance was the only hope
held out to them. If they did not repent, the death
sentence would be executed against them. The
spiritual marriage would then be death-dissolved.

37. God's covenant of wedlock will be completed by
the wedding ceremony for him that "watcheth
[continually], and keepeth [continually] his garments." Isaiah called this attire "garments of salvation" and "robe of righteousness." Jesus said
those without these garments are "naked."

38. Christ stressed conditional salvation all the way
to the end. "Blessed are they that do his commandments, that they may have right to the tree
of life. . . ." Some translate it: "Blessed are they
that cleanse their garments. . . ." Either way, the
right to the tree of life is conditional.

39. We cited 63 Old Testament ifs and 41 New Testament ifs. These 104 if-proofs dealt with the
whole truth about salvation from Genesis to

Revelation. They covered the entire covenant system upon which salvation is based. Our opponents quote only a few texts from scattered parts of the Bible. They have ignored the wholeness of truth and picked a few texts here and there that would fit into their distortion. The twisted mass of doctrinal confusion in Christendom today is the result of this vicious method of interpretation.

40. In the Appendix we listed eight rules of interpretation that have world-wide adoption. They have been universally accepted by courts of law, scientists, logicians, and theologians for many centuries. Our interpretation of the predestination Scriptures satisfies all these rules. The opposing interpretation violates them all.

41. Augustine and Calvin insisted that their opponents on other doctrines obey these rules, but they ignored them in their predestination teaching. They were unfair with the facts.

In my studies of *Calvin's Commentaries* I was particular to note his principles of interpretation and how he argued the meaning of a text. In many places he did it exactly as I have done it. He "despised" the method some use to "twist the Bible . . . to their own liking," and who "turn Scripture this way and that (as they please), and to fool with it as though it were a game; many people have been doing this long enough."

Calvin insisted on "the original meaning of a text." "If everyone has a right to be a judge or arbiter in this matter [of interpretation], nothing can be set down as certain; and our whole religion will be full of uncertainties"—"since there is a danger that fanatical men may rise up and boast rashly that they have the Spirit of God. . . ." Calvin then quoted the proverb: "So many heads, so many minds."

Calvin told interpreters that interpretation "must not be something out of their own heads." He appealed to the *rule of usage*: "Why should they insist on concocting a new interpretation when ordinary usage is against it?" He referred to "Luther indulging his own thoughts too freely" in Biblical interpretation.

On the *rule of unity*, Calvin wrote: "I am compelled to read all these verses together, because otherwise the meaning of the passage will not be clear." On the *rule of historical background,* he wrote: "The prophet's discourse cannot be understood without a knowledge of the history behind it." "We must not torture Scripture into a false meaning."

The above are a few samples that can be found scattered throughout Calvin's writings. The quotations can be verified in *Calvin's Commentaries.*[8]

Calvin used these interpretive principles in his doctrinal disputes with the Papists, Jewish commentators, and doctors at the Sorbonne. He could not have proved his doctrines without them, nor could anyone.

I once discussed some Bible doctrines with an elderly lawyer who was an excellent Bible student. I told him how some expositors interpreted a certain doctrine. He knew about such interpreters, and replied: "They argue it ad absurdum, ad nauseum." This is true of the Eternal Security teachers. After 16 centuries, unconditional salvation remains unproved.

---

[8] Editors, Jos. Haroutunian, Louise P. Smith, V. xxiii, pp. 21, 23, 76, 77, 87, 88, 91, 289, 334, 339. Westminster Press. *Tracts and Treatises on the Doctrine and Worship of the Church*, John Calvin, pp. 478, 481, 482. Eerdmans. 1958.

Eternal Security teachers will not fairly meet a logical objection to their doctrine. They usually resort to evasion and distortion or they give us the old argument: "We are not governed by reason, but by revelation"—when they have neither. The Roman Catholics, false cults, and fanatical groups use the same argument. It would be a happy day for Christian doctrines if many doctrinal teachers could learn to recognize and admit a proved fact when they see it. Many teachers deplore the fact that other teachers have the wrong interpretation when both trample over all fair interpretive laws.

Across the centuries, Augustine and Calvin have confused the world with their inconsistent and self-contradictory words about predestination. The first and most important rule of interpretation is the *rule of definition*. Augustine and Calvin would have been quickly cut down in a court of evidence. Their perplexing language about predestination would not have been tolerated.

Professor Felix Frankfurter of Harvard law school was a Justice of the U.S. Supreme Court from 1939–1962. He was esteemed by his colleagues as "the most important single figure in our whole judicial system." When he died in 1965, our President and nation honored him as "one of the great figures in legal history." One day, when a case was argued, a lawyer was challenged from the bench about the meaning of his words. He replied: "Oh, well, that's just a matter of semantics." Justice Frankfurter snapped:

> Of course. All our work, our whole life is a matter of semantics, because words are the tools with which we work, the material out

of which laws are made, out of which the
Constitution was written. Everything depends
on our understanding of them.[9]

How true! "Everything depends on our understanding of them." If Augustine and Calvin and
others had written with this fact in mind, perhaps there would be less confusion in the doctrinal teachings of America's 260 denominations.
I once heard Justice Frankfurter hand down his
opinion on a question of constitutional law in
the U.S. Supreme Court. It was a model of clarity.

God did not puzzle us about the meaning of
predestination. We are not cast upon a sea of
chance concerning our salvation. In the study
of doctrines, the golden rule is to define the
words, then gather all passages in which the
words occur, and bring them together into har-
mony. The parts are then merged into other
parts. Each fact then fits into other facts. We
find the focus and see the point at which all the
texts converge. Thus, we have united fusion, and
not disunited confusion, as in Eternal Security.

We did this with our 104 proofs, and unconditional salvation is discredited and overthrown
by the conclusive weight of evidence from Genesis to Revelation. Interpretation is serious work.
You can miss a single detail and get a false conclusion.

The Bible is a legal document. It is made up
of covenants. It is full of legal language, ideas,
and illustrations; and Bible covenants must be
understood as human covenants would be understood in a court of law, and that is by the rules
of evidence. Only in this way can they be fairly

---

[9] *Trips to Felix*, The Atlantic Monthly, Garson Kanin, March
1964.

interpreted. False doctrines are misinterpretations. Always remember that sin entered the world after Eve was deceived by believing Satan's misinterpretation of God's plain words.

Many leading authorities agree with Dr. M. S. Terry, who wrote in his masterly work on interpretation:

> The Bible comes to us in the forms of human language, and appeals to our reason and judgment.... It is to be interpreted as we interpret any other volume, by a rigid application of the same laws of language, and the same grammatical analysis.[10]

Dr. Terry said that any interpreter who does not follow this rule is a "dangerous guide."

42. Augustine's predestination leads to despair for many. They ask: "How can I know whether I am predestinated to be saved or predestinated to be damned?" We take these questions to the inspired Paul who said: "Ye are saved if ye keep in memory what I preached unto you...." This is the only way anyone can know he is saved. If Augustine and Calvin, or anyone, believed he could be saved without this condition, he was deceived.

Augustine and Calvin taught that the salvation of the elect is unconditional; but from all the if-evidence we have seen, this unconditional doctrine leads to an absurdity: The elect are saved though they disobey the conditions, and the non-elect are damned though they keep them.

43. Prophecies concerning future Israel tell of a covenant-keeping people: "I will put my laws into their mind, and write them in their hearts: and I will be to them a God, and they shall be to me a people" (Heb. 8: 10). God's preference,

---

[10] *Biblical Hermeneutics*, p. 25. 1895.

past, present, and future, are those who will be to Him a covenant-keeping people, and to whom He can be a Covenant-God.

44. Christ said that none of His sheep will be lost because they continually follow Him. His sheep "shall never perish." No man can pluck them out of the Father's hand (John 10:27–29). These assurances were given to those who follow Christ, but to apply them to those who follow sin is a deception.

We agree with the following statement from Arthur W. Pink who is one of the prominent Calvinist writers:

> We seriously doubt whether there has ever been a time in the history of this Christian era when there were such multitudes of deceived souls within the churches, who verily believe that all is well with their souls when in fact the wrath of God abideth on them.[11]

Many profess salvation who were never saved. Others were saved who did not continue saved. Many non-Calvinists do not believe in Eternal Security, but they act like it, and live like it. They take salvation for granted while they live in continual disobedience to salvation's conditions.

45. The Bible, with all the if-evidence we have seen, rejects the doctrine of unconditional salvation and makes it conditional. Our if-doctrine was used in relation to salvation by God, Moses, Joshua, Samuel, David, Solomon, Isaiah, Jeremiah, Ezekiel, Malachi, Jesus, Paul, Peter, James, and John. Would it be possible to assemble a greater array of evidence to prove anything?

---

[11] *An Exposition of the Sermon on the Mount*, p. 377. Baker, 1959.

46. In proving our case for conditional salvation, we used the same interpretive rules that Augustine and Calvin used on other doctrines, and which they insisted that their opponents also use. Some of our opponents say that our interpretation of Scripture is "legalistic," but hundreds of times throughout the Bible, God spoke of His commandments as "laws," and even elementary students know that to interpret a law we must be legalistic. God was legalistic when He gave His laws.

47. I have given repeated emphasis throughout this book that we cannot earn or merit our salvation, no matter how many conditions we keep. It is only by God's undeserved grace that we are saved.

   "For by grace are ye saved through faith; and that not of yourselves, it is the gift of God: not of works, lest any man should boast" (Eph. 2: 8–9).

   Many struggle helplessly to fulfill their responsibility to obey God's laws but end in defeat. They should read about Paul's spiritual conflict in Romans 7, and then read about the delivering power of the Holy Spirit in Romans 8. Paul said, "I live, yet not I, but Christ *liveth in me*" (Gal. 2: 20). Jesus said we must "abide in the Vine" to receive this flow of divine life. It is only as Christ takes His throne in our hearts and reigns in our lives that His conquering power over sin is released within us.

   Two extremes should be avoided. Some put undue stress on human responsibility and works. Others teach a distorted doctrine about the grace of God. Paul, in Ephesians, presented the side of grace, but James presented the side of faith in action that works under grace. Paul said we must *"continue* in the grace of God" (Acts 13:43). See also Titus 2:11–12.

To all who inquire whether they are predestinated to be saved, the Bible, from Genesis to Revelation, answers: You are saved — if you obey God's conditions for salvation.

Appendix

EIGHT RULES OF INTERPRETATION

For about eight years I have studied and gathered information on the science of interpretation. I searched the world's foremost authorities, both in law and theology. It is a subject of vast importance. Students who read this book will know I've quoted the highest authorities.

This science began at least about 2500 years ago with Socrates and Aristotle who have influenced it to our day.

These eight rules are found in the writings of the foremost legal and Biblical authorities, both ancient and modern. They are found in the writings of Irenaeus, master interpreter among the second-century church fathers. They were used by the master expositors of the Middle Ages all the way to Luther and the Reformation theologians who disproved Romish fallacies with them.

These rules were involved in the great doctrinal debates of the theologians from the Council of Nice (324 A.D.) to the Council of Trent (1545–1563). It is impossible to determine the true meaning of a Bible doctrine without them. There is nothing more important in all Biblical learning than to know these rules and rightly apply them to Bible doctrines.

The doctrinal errors of 19 centuries of church history were violations of these principles. It is also true of all the false doctrines found in Christendom today. Think of any false doctrine you know about and see if it isn't true.

Christian Scientists, Jehovah's Witnesses, Unitarians, and others use these rules in the ordinary affairs of life but they will not apply them to the Scriptures. They would overthrow their doctrines if they did. Calvinists and Seventh-day Adventists use them when it is to their advantage to do so.

These rules are used by all law courts in the Free World. If you should become involved in a court case about the meaning of a Will, Contract, or Deed, the court would use these rules to determine the meaning of the disputed document. In everyday reading and study, everyone uses these rules at times. You could not make sense from anything you read or write if you did not.

Exact rules are needed for an exact result. You cannot get a sure meaning with an uncertain rule. The Bible student must not only study the Scriptures, he must decide *how* he will interpret them. Two persons can read the same texts and get different ideas from them because they put different meanings upon the words.

A doctrine is only as sure as the proof upon which it is established, and it cannot be demonstrated as sure without these rules, which are the principles to which all logical inquiry appeals. It is by a violation of these rules that Eternal Security goes all the way from a false start to a false conclusion.

Many false doctrines are based on a single word or term. Teachers have taken a Biblical word or term and loaded it with a non-biblical meaning. They then detached the word or term from *all* that the Bible teaches about it and built their doctrine on it.

But, "The whole Bible is a Context." No one has the right to speak as an authority on a Bible subject unless he knows *all* that the Bible teaches on that subject. When one applies the rules to all that the Bible teaches about a subject, he stands on proven ground. The Eternal Security teachers have not done this with "predestination."

Dr. G. Campbell Morgan is widely esteemed as "the greatest Bible expositor of the past century," and he said: "We must be set free from the bondage of popular and traditional views in interpretation." [1]

Dr. R. A. Torrey worked with Dwight L. Moody and was the first head of Moody Bible Institute in Chicago. He wrote a valuable book on how to study the Bible, and said that if some Bible teachers "were practicing law and should try in any court of justice to interpret laws, as they interpret the Bible, they would be laughed out of court." [2]

Augustine and Calvin would have been laughed out of court on predestination.

Solomon asked: "Who knoweth the interpretation of a thing?" (Eccles. 8:1). And Peter said that no Scripture "is of any private interpretation" (II Pet. 1:20). No one knows the interpretation of Scripture if he has his own "private" (personal) interpretation. For 19 centuries, interpreters have ignored the rules, forced their private beliefs upon the Scriptures, and claimed to have a revelation from God. This is true of much doctrinal teaching in the world today.

Interpretation is more than knowing a set of rules, but the rules are necessary. The spiritual sense must be derived from the grammatical sense.

---

[1] *Parables and Metaphors*, p. 72.

[2] *The Importance and Value of Proper Bible Study*, p. 67. Moody Press, 1921.

Here are the eight rules:

1. *Rule of Definition*

Any study of Scripture . . . must begin with a study of words. (*Protestant Biblical Interpretation,* Ramm, Bernard, p. 129, W. A. Wilde Co., Boston, 1956)

Define your terms and then keep to the terms defined. (*The Structural Principles of the Bible,* Marsh, F. E., p. 1, Kregel Publications)

In the last analysis, our theology finds its solid foundation only in the grammatical sense of Scripture. The interpreter should . . . conscientiously abide by the plain meaning of the words. (*Principles of Biblical Interpretation,* Berkhof, pp. 74–75, Baker Book House, 1960)

The Bible writers could not coin new words since they would not be understood, and were therefore forced to use those already in use. The content of meaning in these words is not to be determined by each individual expositor . . . to do so would be a method of interpretation [that is] a most vicious thing. (*Studies in the Vocabulary of the Greek New Testament,* Wuest, Kenneth, pp. 30–37, Eerdmans Pub. Co., 1945)

[The author] confines the definitions strictly to their literal or idiomatic force; which, after all, will be found to form the best, and indeed the only safe and solid basis for theological deductions of any kind. (*Young's Analytical Concordance,* Prefatory Note)

2. *Rule of Usage*

The whole Bible may be regarded as written for "the Jew first," and its words and idioms ought to be rendered according to Hebrew usage. (*Synonyms of the Old Testament,* Girdlestone, R. B., p. 14)

Christ then accepted the usage He found existing. He did not alter it. (*Pulpit Commentary,* Matthew, V. 1, xxv, old edition)

Jesus of Nazareth was a Jew, spoke to and moved among Jews in Palestine. . . . He spoke first and directly to the Jews, and His words must have been intelligible to them. . . . It was absolutely necessary to view that Life and Teaching in all its surroundings of place, society, popular life. . . . This would form not only the frame in which to set the picture of the Christ, but the very background of the picture itself. (*The Life and Times of Jesus the Messiah,* Edersheim, Alfred, V. 1, xii, Eerdmans Pub. Co., 1953)

In interpreting very many phrases and histories of the New Testament, it is not so much worth what we think of them from notions of our own . . . as in what sense these things were understood by the hearers and lookers on, according to the usual custom and vulgar dialect of the nation. (*Bishop Lightfoot,* quoted in *The Vocabulary of the Greek New Testament,* xii, Moulton & Milligan, Eerdmans Pub. Co., 1959)

3. Rule of Context

Many a passage of Scripture will not be understood at all without the help afforded by the context; for many a sentence derives all its point and force from the connection in which it stands. (*Biblical Hermeneutics,* Terry, M. S., p. 117. 1896)

[Bible words] must be understood according to the requirements of the context. (*Thayer's Greek-English Lexicon of the New Testament,* p. 97)

Every word you read must be understood in the light of the words that come before and after it. (*How to Make Sense,* Flesch, Rudolph, p. 51, Harper & Brothers, 1954)

[Bible words] when used out of context . . . can prove almost anything. [Some interpreters] twist them . . . from a natural to a non-natural sense. (Irenaeus, second-century church father, quoted in *Inspiration and Interpretation,* p. 50, Eerdmans Pub. Co., 1957)

The meaning must be gathered from the context. (*Encyclopedia Britannica,* Interpretation of Documents, V. 8, p. 912. 1959)

4. *Rule of Historical Background*

Even the general reader must be aware that some knowledge of Jewish life and society at the time is requisite for the understanding of the Gospel history. (*The Life and Times of Jesus the Messiah,* Edersheim, Alfred, V. 1, xiii, Eerdmans Pub. Co., 1953)

The moment the student has in his mind what was in the mind of the author or authors of the Biblical books when these were written, he has interpreted the thought of Scripture. . . . If he adds anything of his own, it is not exegesis. (*International Standard Bible Encyclopedia,* V. 3, p. 1489. 1952)

Theological interpretation and historical investigation can never be separated from each other. . . . The strictest historical . . . scrutiny is an indispensable discipline to all Biblical theology. (*A Theological Word Book of the Bible,* 30 scholars, Preface, Macmillan Co., 1958)

I have said enough to show the part which the study of history necessarily plays in the intelligent study of the law as it is today. . . . Our only interest in the past is for the light it throws upon the present. (U.S. Supreme Court Justice Oliver Wendell Holmes, Jr., 1902–1932, quoted in *The World of Law,* V. 2, p. 630, Simon & Schuster, 1960)

5. *Rule of Logic*

Interpretation is merely logical reasoning. (*Encyclopedia Americana,* V. 15, p. 267. 1953)

The use of reason in the interpretation of Scripture is everywhere to be assumed. The Bible comes to us in the forms of human language, and appeals to our reason . . . it invites investigation, and . . . it is to be interpreted as we interpret any other volume, by a rigid application of the same laws of language, and the same grammatical analysis. (*Biblical Hermeneutics,* Terry, M. S., p. 25. 1895)

What is the control we use to weed out false theological speculation? Certainly the control is logic and evidence . . . interpreters who have not had the sharpening experience of logic . . . may have improper notions of implication and evidence. Too frequently such a person uses a basis of appeal that is a notorious violation of the laws of logic and evidence. (*Protestant Biblical Interpretation,* Ramm, Bernard, pp. 151–153, W. A. Wilde Co., 1956)

It is one of the most firmly established principles of law in England and in America that "a law means exactly what it says, and is to be interpreted and enforced exactly as it reads." This is just as good a principle for interpreting the Bible as for interpreting law. (*The Importance and Value of Proper Bible Study,* Torrey, R. A., pp. 67–70, Moody Press, 1921)

Charles G. Finney, lawyer and theologian, is widely considered the greatest theologian and most successful revivalist since apostolic times. He was often in sharp conflict with the theologians of his day because they violated these rules of interpretation. Finney said he interpreted a Bible passage as he "would have understood the same or like passage in a law book" (*Autobiography,* pp. 42–43) .

Finney stressed the need for definition and logic in theology and said the Bible must be understood on "fair principles of interpretation such as would be admitted in a court of justice" (*Systematic Theology,* Preface, ix) .

6. *Rule of Precedent*

We must not violate the known usage of a word and invent another for which there is no precedent. (*The Greek New Testament for English Readers,* Dean Alford, p. 1098, Moody Press)

The professional ability of lawyers in arguing a question of law, and the judges in deciding it, is thus chiefly occupied with a critical study of previous cases, in order to determine whether the previous cases really support some alleged doctrine. (*Introduction to the Study of Law,* p. 40, Woodruff, E. H., 1898)

The first thing he [the judge] does is to compare the case before him with precedents. ... Back of precedents are the basic juridical conceptions which are postulates of judicial reasoning, and farther back are the habits of life, the institutions of society, in which those conceptions had their origin. ... Precedents have so covered the ground that they fix the point of departure from which the labor of the judge begins. Almost invariably, his first step is to examine and compare them. It is a process of search, comparison, and little more. (U.S. Supreme Court Justice Benjamin Cardozo, 1932–1938, *The Nature of the Judicial Process,* quoted in *The World of Law,* V. 2, p. 671, Simon & Schuster, 1960)

7. *Rule of Unity*

[It is] fundamental to a true interpretation of the Scripture, viz., that the parts of a document, law, or instrument are to be construed with reference to the significance of the whole. (Dean Abbot, *Commentary on Matthew,* Interpretation, p. 31)

Where a transaction is carried out by means of several documents so that together they form part of a single whole, these documents are read together as one. ... [They are to be so read] that, that construction is to be preferred which will render them consistent. (*Interpretation of Documents,* Sir Roland Burrows, p. 49, Butterworth & Co., London, 1946)

8. *Rule of Inference*

In the law of evidence, an inference is a fact reasonably implied from another fact. It is a logical consequence. It is a process of reasoning. It derives a conclusion from a given fact or premise. It is the deduction of one proposition from another proposition. It is a conclusion drawn from evidence. An inferential fact or proposition, although not expressly stated, is sufficient to bind. This principle of interpretation is upheld by law courts. (Jesus proved the resurrection of the dead to the unbelieving Sadducees by this rule—Matt. 22:31, 32. See *Encyclopedia Britannica*, V. 6, p. 615 (1952) and *Black's Law Dictionary*, p. 436, Fourth Edition, West Pub. Co., 1951.)

> A proposition of fact is proved when its truth is established by competent and satisfactory evidence. By competent evidence is meant such evidence as the nature of the thing to be proved admits. By satisfactory evidence is meant that amount of proof which ordinarily satisfies an unprejudiced mind beyond reasonable doubt. Scripture facts are therefore proved when they are established by that kind and degree of evidence which would in the affairs of ordinary life satisfy the mind and conscience of a common man. When we have this kind and degree of evidence it is unreasonable to require more. (*Systematic Theology*, Strong, Augustus H., p. 142, Judson Press, 1899)

It would have been easy to quote many more Biblical and legal authorities on interpretation and evidence, but it would have been needless repetition.